fast & fantastic
food for family & friends

Simon Holst

Acknowledgements

Sincere thanks to all of you who helped get this book off the ground. Special thanks to Hilary and Sam whose efforts helped create the visual feast we have before us, and of course to Lindsay Keats, photographer, who was there to offer his creative input and capture the moment on film.

Thanks, too, to the team at New Holland including freelance designer Gina Hochstein – it may have taken longer than originally anticipated, but I think it was worth it in the end.

Lastly, thanks to my family Sam, Isabella and Theo, who have to live with the creative highs and lows, and to all the friends who have been used (hopefully willingly) as 'guinea pigs' during recipe development and testing.

First published in 2003 by New Holland Publishers (NZ) Ltd
Auckland • Sydney • London • Cape Town

218 Lake Road, Northcote, Auckland, New Zealand
14 Aquatic Drive, Frenchs Forest, NSW 2086, Australia
86–88 Edgware Road, London W2 2EA, United Kingdom
80 McKenzie Street, Cape Town 8001, South Africa

Copyright © 2003 in text: Simon Holst
Copyright © 2003 in photography: Lindsay Keats
Copyright © 2003 New Holland Publishers (NZ) Ltd

ISBN: 1 877246 82 4

Publishing manager: Renée Lang
Design: Gina Hochstein
Editor: Nicky Farquhar
Food styling: Simon Holst
Home economists: Simon Holst, Hilary Wilson-Hill and Sam Ford

A catalogue record for this book is available from the National Library of New Zealand.

10 9 8 7 6 5 4 3 2 1

Colour reproduction by PICA Digital, Singapore
Printed through Bookbuilders, Hong Kong

Cover photograph: Pumpkin, Spinach & Feta Cakes (see page 46)

fast & fantastic
food for family & friends

Simon Holst

photographed by Lindsay Keats

NEW
HOLLAND

contents

introduction

I think that sitting and sharing food with your friends and family is one of life's great pleasures. Sadly, in today's busy world it is easy for cooking – especially cooking for the family – to become just another chore. I really would like to change this attitude and so to try and encourage people to be more enthusiastic I ask them at every opportunity what it is they look for in a cookbook. Almost always the answer is 'food that's quick, easy and interesting'. Many people request healthy options, too – so this is what I have tried to provide here in *Fast & Fantastic*.

In quite a few ways the 'easy and interesting food for busy people' theme of this book is a continuation of that started with its predecessor, *Dish It Up*. But in *Fast & Fantastic*, however, I have switched from an emphasis on one-dish meals (albeit with minimum preparation time) to recipes that can be prepared from start to finish in 60 minutes or less – a bonus for busy lifestyles.

The end result may seem a little eclectic in that it mixes various styles and ethnic influences, but this itself provides versatility. Some of the recipes are intended for 'everyday' weeknight and/or family meals, while others are more elegant and suitable for special occasions. All can be accomplished without being chained to the kitchen for hours beforehand or, worse, during the meal!

I'd like to think that the recipes are simple enough to entice relatively inexperienced cooks to tackle them without fear, but I hope they are also diverse enough to 'push the boundaries' and help expand the repertoires of experienced cooks, too.

I hope this new collection inspires you.

Happy (and relaxed) cooking!

Simon Holst

starters

Pot-Stickers

These delicious dumplings are cooked in an interesting manner. First they are fried to brown their bottoms, the 'pot-sticking' part, then they are steamed. (Ideally, if you use a non-stick pan there should be no sticking at all, but it's easy to see where the name comes from.)

I like to use round, white chiao tzu wrappers (from an Asian-foods store), but if you can't get these, conventional won ton wrappers cut into rounds (with a cookie cutter) will do instead.

For about 30 dumplings:
Filling
1 large clove garlic, peeled
1cm piece fresh ginger
4–5 spring onions, roughly chopped
400g pork mince
2 tablespoons soy sauce
2 teaspoons sesame oil
½ teaspoon sugar
½ teaspoon salt

30 chiao tzu wrappers
2–3 teaspoons canola or olive oil
1–1½ cups hot chicken stock (or
   1 teaspoon instant stock powder
   plus 1 cup hot water)
soy sauce and sweet chilli sauce to
   serve

Place the garlic, ginger and spring onions in a food processor fitted with a metal chopping blade and process until finely chopped. Add the pork and remaining four filling ingredients and process until evenly mixed – don't process more than necessary or you will toughen the mixture. (Alternatively, finely chop the first three ingredients, place in a medium-sized bowl, add next five ingredients and mix thoroughly.)

Place a heaped teaspoon of the filling mixture in the middle of a wrapper (don't be too generous or you won't be able to seal the dumpling). Moisten around the filling with water, then fold the wrapper in half (to make a half moon-shaped package) and gently squeeze the edges together to seal. Sit the dumpling seam up on a board, like a miniature Cornish pastie. Repeat until all the filling is used.

Heat about a teaspoon of the oil in a large non-stick pan. Add as many of the dumplings as will comfortably fit with about 1cm between each and cook over a medium heat for 2–3 minutes or until the bottoms are golden brown. Pour ½ cup of the hot stock into the pan, cover with a close fitting lid and cook for 5–6 minutes until almost all the liquid has gone and the dumplings are cooked through (cut one in half to test). Place the cooked dumplings on a warmed plate and cover with foil while you cook the remaining dumplings.

Arrange the dumplings on individual plates or a platter with small bowls of soy sauce and sweet chilli sauce for dipping and serve while warm.

Pumpkin & Peanut Hummus

Over the past few years there has been a rapid proliferation of different brands and flavours of prepared hummus available on supermarket shelves. I don't know whether this rapid increase in popularity is because hummus is 'healthier' than many other dips and spreads or just because it tastes so good.

Either way I'm always a little surprised that anyone wants to buy the ready-made version when it's so cheap and easy to make your own at home.

For about 1½ cups:

100g peeled and cubed pumpkin
1 large clove garlic, peeled
300g can chickpeas, rinsed and
   drained
¼ teaspoon curry powder
2 tablespoons peanut butter
2 tablespoons lemon juice
2–3 tablespoons olive oil
¼–½ teaspoon salt
water to thin (if required)

Place the cubed pumpkin in a small microwave bowl, cover and microwave on high (100%) for 2 minutes.

While the pumpkin cooks, place the garlic and chickpeas in a blender or food processor, fitted with a metal chopping blade, and process until finely chopped. Add the pumpkin, curry powder, peanut butter and lemon juice. Process until evenly mixed, then add two tablespoons of the oil and ¼ teaspoon of salt. Process until very smooth stopping once or twice to scrape down the sides and adding the extra oil and/or water to thin to the desired consistency, if required. Taste and add a little extra salt if needed.

Serve immediately with warmed pita wedges, crackers and/or vegetable (carrot, cucumber, celery and cauliflower) crudités, or transfer to an air-tight container and store in the fridge for up to a week.

Eggplant & Feta Rolls

These delicious rolls are so simple to make, this is really just a set of assembly instructions, rather than a 'proper' recipe.

I like to use longer thinner eggplants (about 6cm thick), to make small starter-sized rolls, but if you can't get little ones, slices from a larger eggplant can be cut in half once cooked. Alternatively, larger eggplants can be cut more thickly and be used to make larger rolls that can be served as a scrumptious vegetarian main course.

For 10–12 rolls (5–6 servings):

2 small–medium (about 400g total)
   eggplants
3–4 tablespoons olive oil ('plain', basil
   or garlic infused)
1 medium red capsicum (pepper)
100–150g feta cheese
1–2 tablespoons balsamic vinegar
about 2 tablespoons chopped basil
   (or 10–12 basil leaves)
salt and pepper to taste

Cut the eggplants lengthwise into thin (about 7mm) slices. Lightly brush both sides of each slice with oil. Place slices in a preheated contact grill (you may have to do this in several batches) and cook for 4–5 minutes on a high heat or arrange the slices on a non-stick sprayed baking sheet and place them under a preheated grill (5–7cm from the heat) and cook for about 3–4 minutes before turning and cooking a further 3 minutes. Set the cooked eggplants aside until cool enough to handle.

While the eggplants cool, prepare the remaining ingredients. If using a fresh capsicum, cut the flesh from the core in flattish slices, brush these with any remaining oil and cook like the eggplants, then cut into 10–12 strips (you need the same number as you have of slices of eggplant). Cut the feta into the same number of fingers or slices too.

To assemble the rolls, lay a strip of eggplant on a board, brush lightly with balsamic vinegar. Lay a strip of capsicum and a piece of feta across one end, add a little chopped basil or a basil leaf, then sprinkle with salt and pepper then roll up.

Arrange on a serving plate, drizzle with a little extra oil if desired and serve.

Note: *I like to cook the capsicum myself, but if you're short of time, you can use bottled, char-grilled red pepper instead.*

Marinated Feta & Olives

You can buy both marinated feta and a variety of different flavours of marinated olives but it is cheaper and far more satisfying to make your own – the results are impressive for very little effort.

These make good gifts too, but they are not really suitable for long term storage – keep them in the fridge and use within 7–10 days.

For 1 good-sized jar:
Marinated Feta
about 250g feta cheese
1–2 cloves garlic
1 small red chilli
1/2 teaspoon black peppercorns
finely grated rind 1/2 lemon
few sprigs of thyme and rosemary, bruised
canola and olive oil, as required

Cut the feta into bite-sized cubes or chunks (roughly 2cm cubes are good). Peel and halve or roughly chop the garlic cloves and deseed and slice the chilli. Put a layer of feta cubes in the bottom of your jar. (Don t pack them in too tightly or the flavoured oil won t be able to reach all the surfaces.) Add a slice of garlic, a couple of slices of chilli, a few pepper-corns, a pinch of lemon rind and a sprig or two of the herbs. If you want the jar to look its best, poke some of the chilli, garlic and herbs down the side of the jar so you can see them easily.

Continue layering until you have used all the cheese and/or filled the jar. Add any remaining seasonings (unless you are going to start another jar), then two thirds to three quarters fill the jar with canola oil, then fill to the top with olive oil making sure all the cheese is covered. (Canola oil is a light flavourless oil that will carry the olive oil flavours. You can use olive oil only, but it is much more expensive and sometimes turns cloudy when refrigerated.) Put the lid on the jar and invert a few times so the oil and flavourings are mixed.

Leave to stand for at least 15 minutes before serving.

Marinated Olives

about 200g mixed green and Kalamata olives • 4–6 whole cardamom pods, crushed • finely grated rind of 1/2 orange • 1 tablespoon orange juice • canola and olive oil as required

Proceed as above, but replacing the garlic, chilli, lemon rind and herbs with the orange rind and cardamom, and add the orange juice just before filling the jar with canola oil.

Variation: *try using infused/flavoured (say garlic, chilli or basil) olive oil instead of 'plain' for added flavour.*

Crab Dip or Spread

At a glance, this may look like a fairly complicated recipe, but it's really just a case of add everything, mix well, then serve and enjoy.

The crab gives a subtle but interesting flavour to this versatile mixture – chill and serve it as a spread for bread or crackers, or serve it hot (it becomes more liquid) as a dip for crisps, crackers or vegetable crudités.

For about 2 cups:
½ cup cream cheese
¼ cup sour cream
2 spring onions, finely chopped
2 sticks (about ¼ cup) celery, finely
    diced
1 clove garlic, crushed, peeled and
    chopped
2 tablespoons lemon juice
1 tablespoon horseradish sauce
1 tablespoon sweet chilli sauce
1 teaspoon finely grated lemon rind
1 teaspoon Worcestershire sauce
1 teaspoon fish sauce
2 x 170g cans crab meat
¼ teaspoon hot chilli sauce to taste
salt and pepper to taste

Measure the cream cheese and sour cream into a medium-sized bowl and stir until smooth. Add the next nine ingredients and mix until well combined.

Open and drain the cans of crab meat, then fold the meat into the dip mixture. Season to taste with the hot chilli sauce, salt and pepper.

Refrigerate before serving as a spread, or, warm it in the microwave (or on the stovetop) and serve as a delicious dip.

For something really different, spoon it into small individual ramekins, and brown the tops under a hot grill before serving.

Chicken Liver Pâté

I have to confess that I'm usually more than a little squeamish about handling (and eating) offal. I will however make an exception for this smooth, creamy, chicken liver pâté.

For 1½–2 cups:
50g butter
2 cloves garlic
1 teaspoon chopped fresh thyme
    (or ½ teaspoon dried thyme)
400–500g chicken livers
¼ cup sherry
½–1 teaspoon salt
pepper to taste

Melt the butter in a medium–large frypan. Add the garlic and thyme and cook for 1–2 minutes, stirring frequently.

Tip the chicken livers into the pan and cook over a medium heat, stirring and turning them frequently (breaking up the larger livers so they cook more quickly), for about 5 minutes, or until the largest livers are no longer pink in the centres when cut in half.

Allow the mixture to cool for a few minutes, then transfer the livers and liquid to a food processor fitted with a metal chopping blade, and process until finely chopped. Add the sherry, salt and a grind of pepper, then process until smooth.

Pour half the pâté mixture into a sieve held over a medium-sized pot or bowl (the finer the sieve, the smoother the finished pâté). Gently shake the sieve from side to side and/or jiggle the sieve up and down, tapping its rim on the edge of the pot, until the mixture has passed through. Rinse and dry the sieve (discarding the coarse bits) if it is looking clogged, then repeat with the other half of the mixture.

Transfer the pâté into serving dishes or small airtight containers and store in the fridge until required.

Mushroom & Almond Pâté

As is probably the goal for any pâté, the flavours of the almonds, mushrooms and onion in this really do merge to produce something quite different, slightly unexpected and delicious, with no one flavour dominating.

It is not necessarily the goal when making any vegetarian dish, but, intentionally or not, this tasty pâté could easily (at least in terms of colour and appearance) be mistaken for a liver-based version.

For about 1¹/₂ cups:

1 cup whole, unblanched almonds
2 tablespoons olive oil
1 medium onion, peeled and finely
   chopped
2 cloves garlic, crushed, peeled and
   chopped
150g brown button mushrooms, sliced
2 tablespoons chopped basil
¹/₄ teaspoon dried thyme
¹/₂ teaspoon salt
¹/₄ cup sherry

Preheat the oven to 180°C. Spread the almonds on a sponge roll tin and cook for 10–12 minutes or until they just begin to colour.

While the almonds cook, heat the oil in a medium frypan. Add the onion and garlic and cook, stirring occasionally, until the onion is soft and clear, then add the mushrooms. Continue to cook, stirring frequently, for 2–3 minutes longer until the mushrooms have softened and wilted, then remove from the heat and stir in the herbs, salt and sherry.

Cool the cooked nuts for a few minutes, then tip them into a food processor fitted with a metal chopping blade. Process until the nuts are finely chopped (about the size of breadcrumbs), then add the mushroom and onion mixture. Process again until the mixture is smooth and creamy. Serve immediately as you would any pâté or transfer to a clean, airtight container and store in the fridge for up to a week.

Chilli-Soy Roasted Almonds

Nuts make a great snack to enjoy with drinks, or in fact at any time of the day. Not only do they taste good, but there is increasing evidence that they are good for you – they actually appear to help protect against heart disease.

Although I think even whole raw almonds are delicious, they are even better and more satisfying when cooked. Roasted like this they contain a minimal amount of added fat (especially compared with bought 'roasted' nuts, which are usually fried), so you can just relax and enjoy!

For about 2 cups:

2 cups whole, unblanched almonds
4 teaspoons Kikkoman or other light
   soy sauce
1 tablespoon sesame oil
1 teaspoon hot chilli sauce

Preheat the oven to 160°C. Measure the almonds into a medium-sized bowl, add the soy sauce, oil, and chilli sauce, then stir to combine.

Allow the nuts to stand for a few minutes, then spread them on a teflon or baking paper-lined sponge roll tin. Place them in the oven (just above the middle) and cook for 10–12 minutes, stirring once or twice to prevent burning, or until lightly browned and plump looking.

Remove from the oven and cool before storing in an airtight container until required.

Babaganoush

I think eggplant is delicious, but I know there are those out there who are not so convinced of its merits. Even if you're not a great eggplant fan, you should try this tasty dip – it's really easy to make, and if you didn't know what went in, I don't think you would ever actually guess.

Serve it with wedges of warmed pita bread or vegetable crudités like any dip or perhaps as part of a mezze platter with some marinated feta and/or olives on the side.

For about 1½ cups:
1 medium eggplant (300–400g)
1 medium–large clove garlic, peeled
2–3 tablespoons lemon juice
2 tablespoons tahini
3–4 tablespoons olive oil
about ½ teaspoon salt

Prick the eggplant with a skewer in several places, then microwave it whole on high (100%) for 4–5 minutes, turning it over after 2 minutes, until it is soft and wrinkly. (Alternatively, place the eggplant in an oven pre-heated to 180°C and bake for 35–45 minutes, until soft and wrinkly.)

Once the eggplant is cool enough to handle, place on a chopping board, cut in half and scrape the flesh out of the skin. Place the flesh in a food processor fitted with the metal chopping blade, add the garlic, lemon juice and tahini and process until smooth.

With the motor running, drizzle in the olive oil and add the salt. Stop the processor, taste the mixture and a little more salt if required.

Serve immediately, or transfer to an airtight container and refrigerate for up to a week.

Note: *tahini is a paste made from ground sesame seeds. Look for it in the refrigerated foods section of larger supermarkets – it's often with the pre-prepared dips etc.*

Tzatziki

There is something inherently cooling and soothing about the flavour of cucumber, so it is easy to understand how this smooth and creamy mixture evolved under the hot Mediterranean sun.

The combination of cucumber and yoghurt just seems to crop up again and again, so it's not surprising that tzatziki, despite its simple combination of grated cucumber and yoghurt, with a little garlic thrown in for good measure, is so good.

For about 1½ cups:
2 cups plain unsweetened yoghurt or
  1 cup thick Greek-style yoghurt
about ½ medium telegraph (thin
  skinned seedless) cucumber
1 large clove garlic, crushed, peeled
  and chopped
½ teaspoon salt
extra virgin olive oil to drizzle (optional)

Line a large sieve with a clean tea towel or a double layer of cheesecloth. Pour in the yoghurt and leave to stand over a bowl for 20–30 minutes, then gather up the corners of the cloth and squeeze the yoghurt gently. It is surprising how much 'excess' liquid this can remove, leaving the yoghurt thick and creamy. (Omit this step if using Greek-style yoghurt.)

Halve the cucumber lengthways, then scrape out (and discard) the seeds using a teaspoon. Coarsely grate the cucumber flesh, gather it up and, holding it over the sink, squeeze gently to get rid of any excess liquid.

Combine the yoghurt, cucumber, garlic and salt in a medium-sized bowl. Stir gently to combine and it's ready to serve. The creamy white flecked with darker green looks (and tastes) good drizzled with greenish extra virgin olive oil if desired.

Serve as a dip or spread for warmed pita or crusty bread.

Spicy Fish Cakes

These make a great appetiser to pass around with drinks as a pre-dinner snack. Alternatively, if you come to like them as much as I do, they can be served with rice and salad as a main.

Serve with the tangy dipping sauce given below and/or little bowls of Thai sweet chilli sauce.

For about 20 cakes:
3 slices white bread
1/2 medium red onion, peeled
300–400g fish fillets, roughly chopped
2 teaspoons red curry paste
1 tablespoon fish sauce
1 teaspoon sesame oil
1/2 teaspoon salt
1/2 teaspoon sugar
about 1/4 cup chopped coriander
1 medium carrot, grated
2–3 tablespoons olive or canola oil for
    frying

Dipping Sauce
2 tablespoons lime or lemon juice
1 tablespoon fish sauce
1 tablespoon water
1 teaspoon sugar
finely chopped red chilli to taste
tiny cubes of carrot and chopped
    coriander for colour

Tear the bread slices into 4–6 pieces each and place in a food processor fitted with a metal chopping blade. Process until the bread is in crumbs no larger than peas.

Chop the onion into 4–6 chunks and add to the crumbs along with the fish. Process until the fish is finely chopped, then add the next five ingredients and process until the mixture begins to form a ball. Add the coriander and carrot and process until just mixed.

Working with wet hands (this prevents sticking), shape the mixture into walnut-sized balls, then flatten these into disks about 1½cm thick. When the cakes are shaped, set them aside for a couple of minutes while you prepare the dipping sauce by combining all the ingredients in a small bowl and stirring until the sugar dissolves.

Heat just enough of the oil to cover the bottom of a non-stick frypan. Add as many of the cakes as will comfortably fit in one batch and cook over a medium heat until the first side is golden brown (about 3 minutes), then gently turn them over and cook the second side.

Remove from the pan and drain on paper towels while you cook the rest. Arrange on a platter (thinly shredded lettuce makes a good base) with a bowl (or bowls) of the dipping sauce and serve.

Cigar Borek – Cigarette Pies

These are based on simple but delicious little pies I had in Turkey – needless to say these are named for their shape, not their feta-based contents!

For 12 little 'pies':
100g feta cheese, crumbled
1/4 cup chopped parsley
1 tablespoon lemon juice
3–6 sheets filo pastry
1–2 tablespoons olive oil

Preheat the oven to 180°C. While the oven heats, combine the crumbled feta, parsley and lemon juice in a small bowl.

Trim the filo sheets so they are square, then cut these into quarters to make smaller squares. Place a small square on a board and brush lightly with oil, then cover with a second sheet. Arrange a scant tablespoon of the filling mix diagonally across the square just below the middle (don t be too generous or you may run out and they may burst during cooking). Fold in three corners to cover the filling (so it looks like an open envelope), then roll up towards the open point.

Arrange the pies on a tray, brush lightly with oil and bake for 8–10 minutes until golden brown. Serve hot or warm.

soups

Moroccan-Style Chickpea & Chicken Soup

This soup, alone or with bread, makes a substantial meal for 4–6 adults. Alternatively you could serve it as a delicious starter for a Moroccan-themed meal for a considerably larger group.

For 4–6 servings:

2 tablespoons olive or canola oil
about 400g (2 large) skinless, boneless chicken breasts
1 medium–large onion
1 large carrot
1 teaspoon ground cumin
1 teaspoon ground coriander
1/2 teaspoon ground turmeric
1/2 teaspoon chilli flakes or powder
1 cinnamon stick
2 x 400g cans diced tomatoes in juice
4 cups chicken stock
2 x 300g can chickpeas, rinsed and drained
1 teaspoon paprika
1 lemon, zest and juice
1/2–1 teaspoon salt
3–4 tablespoons chopped coriander

Heat the oil in a large pot or casserole dish. Add the chicken breast and cook over a high heat for 2 minutes a side until lightly browned, then remove chicken and set aside.

While the chicken cooks, peel, quarter and slice the onion and dice the carrot. Once the chicken has been browned (and removed) add the onion and carrot to the pot and cook, stirring occasionally, for 3–5 minutes until the onion has softened and is beginning to brown. Stir in the cumin, coriander, turmeric, chilli and the cinnamon stick and cook, stirring continuously, for another minute.

Pour in the tomatoes (and their juice), stock, and chickpeas. Add the chicken breasts back to the soup, stir in the paprika, lemon zest and juice and salt to taste. Bring to the boil then reduce the heat to a simmer and cook for 20–25 minutes. Remove and cool the chicken breasts then shred them using two forks or clean hands.

Stir the shredded meat and most of the coriander (reserve a little for garnishing) into the soup and serve. A crusty loaf or warmed flat breads make ideal accompaniments and a teaspoon or so of sour cream and a little chopped coriander or parsley give an attractive (and tasty) finishing touch.

Roasted Corn & Capsicum Soup

This soup provides a happy marriage between the cooler autumn weather and the bounty of late summer. The corn adds sweetness, substance and texture, while the peppers add flavour and a lovely rosy blush to what would otherwise be a fairly pale looking soup.

The ingredients and seasonings used give this soup a distinctly Tex-Mex flavour, and in keeping with this I like to add a little bit of chilli powder, but this is completely optional. A little smoked paprika (available in tins from delicatessens) gives a slightly smoky flavour, but this too can be omitted without serious consequences.

For about 6 servings:

2 red capsicums (peppers)
4 whole ears of corn
1 tablespoon canola or olive oil
1 medium onion
1 clove garlic
1 teaspoon ground cumin
1/2 teaspoon oregano
1/4–1/2 teaspoon chilli powder (to taste)
1/2 teaspoon smoked (or regular) paprika (optional)
4 cups chicken or vegetable stock (or 4 cups hot water, plus 3 teaspoons instant stock powder)
salt and pepper to taste
1–2 tablespoons chopped coriander or parsley

Preheat the oven to 200°C. Halve the capsicums lengthways and remove the seeds and stalks. Place the capsicums cut side down in a large non-stick sprayed roasting pan. Arrange the corn (husks and all) around the capsicums then place in the oven and roast for 30 minutes.

Remove the roasted vegetables from the oven and as soon as the capsicums are cool enough to handle, place them in a plastic bag and leave to stand for a further 5–10 minutes (this helps to further loosen the skins). While the corn and capsicums cool, heat the oil in a large pot and peel and chop or dice the onion and peel and chop the garlic. Cook the onion and garlic in the oil until soft, stirring frequently to prevent browning. Add the cumin, oregano, chilli powder and paprika (if using), cook for a minute longer, then remove from the heat.

Pull off and discard the capsicum skins (they should lift off quite easily). Place the capsicum flesh, onion mixture and 1 cup of stock in a food processor fitted with a metal chopping blade and process to a smooth purée. Transfer the purée back to the pot.

Peel and discard the husks and silk from the corn, and slice the kernels from the cobs. Place half of the kernels and 1 cup of stock in the food processor and process until smooth, before adding to the pot. Repeat this process with the remaining corn before rinsing the processor with the final cup of stock.

Season to taste with salt and pepper, add the coriander or parsley, then simmer for a few minutes before serving.

Crusty bread rolls or cornbread make ideal accompaniments.

Mexican Beef, Lime & Tortilla Soup

This spicy soup makes an interesting and warming meal in cooler weather. Corn tortillas may sound like an unusual addition to a soup, but after simmering in it for a while they actually soften and swell, becoming quite pasta-like.

For 4 servings:

2 tablespoons olive or canola oil
1 large onion, peeled and diced
2 cloves garlic, crushed, peeled and chopped
1 medium green capsicum (pepper)
500g lean minced beef
2 teaspoons ground cumin
1 teaspoon ground coriander
1/2–1 teaspoon chilli powder to taste
1/2 teaspoon oregano
2–3 medium tomatoes, diced
4 cups chicken stock
6 soft corn tortillas
juice 2 limes or lemons
1/2–1 teaspoon salt
1/4 cup chopped coriander
1–2 tablespoons olive or canola oil

Heat the oil in a large pot. Stir in the onion and garlic and cook, stirring frequently, for 3–5 minutes until the onion is soft and just beginning to brown. While the onion cooks, core and dice the capsicum. Add the capsicum and minced beef to the pot and cook, stirring occasionally, for about 5 minutes until the beef is lightly browned. Sprinkle in the cumin, coriander and chilli powder and cook, stirring frequently, for about 1 minute longer.

Add the oregano, tomatoes and the stock. Bring the soup to the boil, then reduce the heat to a simmer and cook for about 10 minutes longer. While the soup simmers, rip or cut 5 tortillas into pieces about 2 1/2 x 2 1/2cm square.

Stir the tortilla pieces, lime or lemon juice (lime gives it a particularly 'fresh' flavour) and salt to taste into the soup. Simmer for about 5 minutes longer, then stir in most of the chopped coriander.

To make an attractive garnish, cut the remaining tortilla into strips about 5mm wide. Heat the second measure of oil in a medium non-stick pan, add the tortilla strips and cook until golden brown, then remove them from the pan and drain on paper towels (they will crisp up as they cool).

Serve immediately, garnished with the crisp tortilla strips and the reserved chopped coriander. An avocado and tomato salad and perhaps some additional warmed tortillas make excellent accompaniments.

Note: *soft (i.e. not fried or baked until crisp) corn tortillas used to be relatively hard to come by, but now they can be found vacuum packed in the Mexican foods section of most supermarkets.*

French Onion Soup

Whenever I make this classic soup, I wonder why I don't make it more often. It is quick and simple to make, especially if you have a food processor, and versatile. It makes a good starter for a more formal meal or, if you add the cheesy croutons, it is quite capable of forming the basis of a more casual meal.

For 4–6 servings:
1kg (about 5 medium) onions
2 tablespoons olive or canola oil
2 tablespoons balsamic vinegar
½–1 teaspoon dried thyme
4 cups vegetable or chicken stock
½–1 cup dry white wine
about 1 teaspoon salt
pepper to taste

Halve, peel and thinly slice the onions (a food processor fitted with the slicing blade does this very efficiently). Heat the oil in a large, heavy pot then add the onions. Cook, stirring frequently, until the onions have softened and are beginning to brown (about 10–15 minutes), then add the balsamic vinegar and the thyme. Continue to cook, stirring frequently and watching closely so the onion doesn't catch on the bottom and burn, until the mixture is well browned (this browning gives the soup much of its final colour and flavour).

Stir in the stock and wine and season to taste. Bring the mixture to the boil, then reduce the heat and simmer gently for a further 15–20 minutes. Check the seasonings again, then serve. Add Cheesy Croutons (see below) and a green salad on the side to make a really easy meal.

Cheesy Croutons

The traditional way to prepare these is to ladle the soup into individual bowls, cover the top of each with sliced bread and sprinkle generously with grated cheese. The bowls are then placed under the grill until the cheese is golden brown.

To avoid having to get hot soup-filled bowls in and out of the oven, I prefer to cheat, and just make the croutons separately. Simply arrange sliced bread on a baking sheet, grill the first side until golden, then turn them over, sprinkle them with grated cheese and grill them again until golden brown. These croutons can then be floated on top of the individual bowls or just served alongside the soup.

Chorizo & Bean Soup

I'm not a 'simmer for hours' type of soup maker. When I do make soup I like to have something substantial enough to serve as a meal in its own right in a relatively short space of time.

For 4 (main course) servings:
2 tablespoons olive or canola oil
1 medium–large onion, peeled and
    diced
2 cloves garlic, crushed, peeled and
    chopped
1 medium potato
1 medium carrot
2 sticks celery, thinly sliced
200g chorizo sausages, thinly sliced
2 x 400g cans cannellini beans, rinsed
    and drained
1 can chicken consommé plus 2½
    cups water or 4 cups chicken stock
½ teaspoon dried thyme
½ teaspoon dried basil
½–1 teaspoon salt
pepper to taste
3–4 tablespoons chopped parsley

Heat the oil in a large pot. Add the onion and garlic and cook, stirring frequently to prevent browning, until the onion has softened. While the onion cooks, scrub the unpeeled potato and carrot and finely dice (the smaller the dice, the faster they will cook). Stir these into the pot along with the celery and chorizo and continue to cook, stirring frequently, for 3–4 minutes longer, until the chorizo begins to brown.

Tip in the beans and consommé and water or the stock, then sprinkle in the basil and thyme. Bring the mixture to the boil, then reduce the heat to a simmer and cook for 10–15 minutes, stirring occasionally.

Taste the soup and season with salt and pepper. (The quantity of salt required will depend on how salty the chorizo were). Stir in most of the parsley, reserving a little to use as a garnish, and cook for a few minutes longer before serving.

Crusty bread and a side salad are all that are required to turn this into a complete, delicious and satisfying meal.

Note: *You can substitute any white beans (butter beans etc) or even chickpeas for cannellini beans, and exact can size does not matter, you could use three 300g cans if they're all you can get.*

Watercress Soup with Smoked Salmon

This smooth, creamy soup makes a stylish first course for an elegant dinner party.

For 4–6 servings:
1 medium onion
1 clove garlic
1 tablespoon olive or canola oil
1 medium potato, peeled and diced
1 cup hot water
3 cups fish stock
2–3 cups lightly packed watercress
1/2 cup cream
1/2–1 teaspoon salt
pepper to taste
nutmeg to taste
about 30g smoked salmon per serving
finely chopped chives to garnish

Peel and finely dice the onion and crush, peel and chop the garlic. Heat the oil in a large pot, add the onion and garlic and cook until soft, stirring frequently so they do not brown. Stir in the potato and cook for a couple of minutes longer, then add the water and fish stock. Simmer for 10–15 minutes or until the potato is very tender, then add the watercress and simmer for a few minutes longer until this too is wilted and tender.

Transfer the mixture to a blender or food processor (you may have to do this in two or three batches) and process until very smooth. Pour the processed soup back into the pot and add the cream (pour it through a sieve if you want to be doubly sure there are no lumps), then season to taste with salt, pepper and a little freshly ground nutmeg. Reheat and simmer gently for a few minutes before serving.

To serve, ladle the hot soup into warmed, shallow soup bowls. Gently press a little smoked salmon (about 30g per serving is plenty) into a small bowl, or even a shot glass, and invert and unmold this into the bowl to form an island in the middle. Garnish with some chopped chives and serve.

Roast Pumpkin & Garlic Soup

Essentially, this soup involves nothing more complicated than roasting some vegetables and making a white sauce, neither of which can be considered particularly arduous or involved.

For 6–8 servings:
1kg peeled and deseeded pumpkin
1 medium onion, peeled and quartered
2 medium carrots, quartered
1 red capsicum (pepper), quartered
   and deseeded
2 x 5cm sprigs rosemary
3–4 x 5cm sprigs thyme
2–3 tablespoons olive or other oil
1 head garlic
2 tablespoons butter
2 tablespoons flour
1 cup milk
3–4 cups chicken or vegetable stock
   (or 3–4 cups water plus 2 teaspoons
   instant stock powder)
salt and pepper to taste
cream to garnish
chopped chives to garnish

Preheat the oven to 200°C. Put the first six ingredients in a plastic bag, add the oil and toss/shake the bag so they are evenly coated with the oil. Slice the top few millimetres off the whole head of garlic then drizzle it with about 1 teaspoon of oil and wrap it tightly in a square of foil. Tip the vegetables into a large roasting pan, add the garlic and cook for 30 minutes until soft and browned around the edges. Remove from the oven and leave to stand until cool enough to handle.

Melt the butter in a large pot. Stir in the flour, cook for about a minute, stirring continuously, then add the milk. Allow the mixture to boil and thicken, whisking to remove any lumps, then remove from the heat.

Unwrap the garlic and squeeze the softened contents from the papery skin into a food processor. Remove and discard the skin from the capsicum pieces and then place in the processor along with a third to half the other vegetables (depending on the size of your processor). Process until smooth adding 1/2–1 cup of stock as required. Transfer the purée to the pot and repeat the process with the remaining vegetables.

Stir the pot to combine, adding the remaining stock until the soup has reached the consistency you like. Season to taste with salt and pepper. Serve immediately or reheated as required, garnished with a swirl of cream and some chopped fresh chives.

Asian-style Meatball & Noodle Soup

I think my love of Asian-style soups stretches back to my childhood, when for a special treat Mum and Dad would take us out to dinner at a local Chinese restaurant. The one item that I can always remember ordering was 'Long and Short Soup', a clear broth full of long noodles and deliciously slippery wontons.

I think this soup captures many of the same flavours and textures, without having to go to the trouble of making wontons first. Served in large bowls, this soup can easily serve as the main part of a meal.

For 2–3 servings:
Broth
2 cups chicken stock
2 cups water
2 dried Chinese (shiitake) mushrooms
2 1/2cm piece ginger, quartered
1 tablespoon light soy sauce

Meatballs
1 clove garlic, peeled
2 1/2cm piece ginger, peeled and
  roughly chopped
2 tablespoons chopped coriander
400g pork mince
2 teaspoons cornflour
1 large egg
1 tablespoon light soy sauce
2 teaspoons sesame oil

100–150g rice noodles (sticks)
1 large carrot, peeled and finely
  julienned
about 20 (100g total) spinach leaves or
  1 cup thinly sliced cabbage
1–2 tablespoons chopped coriander

Combine the ingredients for the broth in a large pot, then place on the stove to boil.

To make the meatballs, put the garlic, ginger and coriander in a food processor fitted with a metal chopping blade. Process until finely chopped, then add the mince, broken into 4–6 smaller lumps, the cornflour, egg, soy sauce and sesame oil. Process in short bursts until evenly mixed.

Working with wet hands (this prevents the mixture sticking), form the meat mixture into 10–12 roughly golf ball-sized balls. Carefully drop the balls into the boiling broth mixture, and boil gently for about 10 minutes, turning the meatballs two or three times as they cook.

While the meatballs cook, prepare the rice noodles by placing them in a large bowl or pot and cover with boiling water. Leave to stand for 5 minutes, or until tender, then drain and set aside. Prepare the carrot and spinach or cabbage. When the meatballs are cooked through (cut one in half after 10 minutes to check), add the vegetables to the pot and cook for 1–2 minutes longer until they have softened, then stir in the chopped coriander.

The soup can be served in two ways, either add the noodles to the pot (a good idea if they have cooled) then ladle into bowls along with everything else, or divide them directly between the serving bowls to be topped with the steaming broth and other goodies. Serve immediately and enjoy!

Lemongrass & Lime Leaf-scented Chicken Soup

Lemongrass and kaffir lime leaves give this soup a wonderful, almost perfume-like fragrance and a fresh flavour. The chilli (I use dried Thai chillies that are about 7–10cm long and are actually quite mild) is removed before serving and just adds a little depth without adding any real heat.

If you're not familiar with kaffir lime leaves, they are available dried from stores specialising in Asian foods, however, increasingly they can also be found fresh in small packets. Although more expensive, if you can find the fresh leaves, they have a better flavour and aroma. (If you can't find either, lemon leaves give an interesting flavour, although not as intense or aromatic.)

For 3–4 servings:
1 medium onion
2 tablespoons canola oil
2 stalks lemongrass, bruised
3–4 kaffir lime leaves
1 whole dried chilli
5cm cinnamon stick
400–500g skinless, boneless chicken
    breast, sliced
4 cups chicken stock
1 tablespoon light soy sauce
1/2 teaspoon each sugar and salt
3/4 cup coconut cream
1 medium carrot, julienned
100g bean thread or rice vermicelli
2–3 tablespoons fresh coriander
about 1 cup bean sprouts

Peel, quarter and slice the onion while the oil heats in a large pot. Stir the sliced onion into the pot and cook for 2–3 minutes, stirring occasionally, until the onion has softened but not browned.

Add the lemongrass, lime leaves, chilli, cinnamon stick and chicken and stir-fry for a couple of minutes, until the chicken is no longer pink on the outside, then add the stock, soy sauce, sugar and salt.

Simmer gently for about 5 minutes or until the chicken is just cooked through, then add the coconut cream, carrot, and vermicelli. Ensure all the vermicelli is under the liquid, then cover and simmer for about 5 minutes longer or until the noodles are tender through. Remove and discard the chilli, cinnamon stick and lemongrass stalks.

Stir in most of the coriander, reserving a little to use as a garnish. Taste and add a little extra salt if required, then divide between serving bowls. Top each bowl with a small handful of bean sprouts and a little of the reserved coriander, then serve. (Roti or naan breads make good accompaniments if serving as a meal.)

Fatoush with Lamb

There's something about this delicious salad that just screams summer. The pita breads are an unusual and interesting addition – shortly after the salad is made they are slightly crunchy, but as the salad stands they soak up some of the juices and become almost meaty – either way they're good.

For 4 servings:
500g lamb rump
1 tablespoon lemon juice
1 tablespoon olive oil
1 teaspoon ground cumin
1 teaspoon paprika
4 medium (about 300g total) pita
   breads
4 medium tomatoes
½ medium telegraph (thin
   skinned seedless) cucumber
1 green capsicum, cored, quartered
   and sliced
½ medium red onion, thinly sliced
½ cup chopped mixed coriander and
   mint
½ teaspoon sugar
salt and pepper to taste
3 tablespoons lemon juice
2 tablespoons olive oil

Preheat the oven to 200°C. Place the lamb in a plastic bag with the lemon juice, oil, cumin and paprika and leave to marinate.

When the oven is hot, remove the lamb from the plastic bag, place on a roasting pan and cook for 12–15 minutes, depending on the thickness of the rump and how well you like it cooked. Remove from the oven and leave to stand for 5–10 minutes before carving into slices about 5mm thick.

While the lamb cooks, spread the pita breads on another tray and place these in the oven until they begin to crisp up (about 5 minutes), then remove them from the oven. When they are cool enough to handle, cut or tear them into bite-sized wedges.

Cut each tomato into 6–8 chunks and place these in a large salad bowl. Halve the cucumber lengthways and scoop out and discard the seeds, then cut the flesh into bite-sized chunks and add to the bowl along with the sliced capsicum, onion and chopped herbs.

Add the sliced lamb and pita bread wedges to the bowl and gently toss everything together. Sprinkle in the sugar and add salt and pepper to taste, drizzle with the lemon juice and olive oil, then toss again. Taste and adjust seasonings if required, then serve.

Surimi & Rice Salad with Lemon & Wasabi Dressing

Some people turn their noses up at the thought of surimi but I think it has several features that make it quite interesting. First, it is inexpensive and second, it is pre-cooked – an especially useful attribute when it comes to making salads on evenings when you just can't quite muster the energy to cook.

I like the flavour too, and think that the lemon and wasabi dressing gives it a real lift, giving the whole salad a light summery feel.

For 2–3 main servings:
Salad
1 cup short or medium grain rice
2 cups boiling water
1/2 teaspoon salt
1 medium green pepper, diced
1 medium carrot, diced
about 1/2 cup diced daikon (optional)
2–3 sticks celery, thinly sliced
2 spring onions, thinly sliced
about 400g surimi

Dressing
1 lemon, zest and juice
2–3 teaspoons wasabi paste
1/4 cup canola oil
1/2 teaspoon each sugar and salt
pepper to taste

Measure the rice, water and salt into a medium-sized microwave bowl, cover and microwave on medium (50%) for 16 minutes or until the rice is tender.

While the rice cooks prepare the vegetables and mix them in a large bowl. Chop or tear the surimi into easily manageable pieces and add to the vegetables.

To make the dressing, finely grate the rind from half the lemon then squeeze and collect all the juice. Whisk together the lemon rind and juice, wasabi (wasabi is hot so if you are in any doubt start with the smaller amount and add more if you think it is required), oil, sugar and salt. Season with pepper to taste.

Leave the cooked rice to cool to about room temperature (if you're in a hurry spread it out on a tray or board), then add it to the vegetable-surimi mixture. Pour in the dressing and stir gently until evenly mixed. Serve as is or accompany with crusty bread.

Thai-Style Chicken Salad

This is a really versatile mixture! It can be served warm or cool, or even chilled – either just as it is, with rice if you want to make it more substantial, or even stretched with some additional salad greens as a filling for tasty bread rolls.

For 3–4 servings:
1 tablespoon canola oil
1 clove garlic, crushed, peeled and
    chopped
1 tablespoon finely chopped ginger
1 stalk lemongrass
400–500g minced chicken
1–2 teaspoons minced red chilli
2 tablespoons lime or lemon juice
2 tablespoons fish sauce
1/2 medium red onion, sliced
    lengthways
1/4–1/2 cup roughly chopped coriander
2 cups mesclun

Heat the oil in a large, non-stick pan. Add the garlic and ginger and cook, stirring frequently, for about a minute.

Peel any tough outside leaves from the lemongrass and finely chop the tender base (usually about 4–5cm), discarding the rest. Stir the lemongrass, then the chicken into the pan and cook, stirring frequently to break up any lumps, for about 5 minutes. Stir in the minced chilli to taste and cook for 1–2 minutes longer, then remove the pan from the heat.

Transfer the chicken mixture to a large bowl and stir in the lime or lemon juice, fish sauce and onion. When the chicken mixture has cooled so it is just warm add the coriander (don't worry about the seemingly large quantity, it should be almost like another salad green) and the mesclun leaves. Toss gently to combine and serve.

Note: *If you are working in advance, prepare the chicken mixture then refrigerate until required, adding the greens just before serving.*

Chicken & Rice Salad

At a glance this salad may seem complicated, but it really only takes about 20 minutes to prepare from start to finish, and it can definitely stand alone as the main part of a meal.

For 4 servings:

1 cup basmati or jasmine rice
2 cups boiling water
1/2 teaspoon salt
1 cup water
1/4 cup light soy sauce
2 cloves garlic, crushed, peeled and chopped
1cm piece ginger, peeled and chopped
1/2 teaspoon five-spice powder
400–500g skinless, boneless chicken breasts
1 medium carrot, peeled and diced
1 medium zucchini, diced
2 sticks celery, thinly sliced
1/2 cup frozen peas
2 medium spring onions (whites and greens), chopped
1/2 cup lightly roasted almonds or cashews for serving
2–3 tablespoons chopped coriander to garnish

Dressing

1/2 cup chicken cooking liquid
2 tablespoons canola oil
2 tablespoons white wine vinegar
1/2 teaspoon each sugar and salt

Measure the rice into a large microwave bowl. Add the boiling water and salt, then cover and microwave on medium (50%) for 15 minutes.

While the rice cooks, combine the next five ingredients in a large pot or lidded frypan and heat to boiling. Halve the chicken breasts lengthways (this will help them cook faster) and add them to the pot or pan. Bring the mixture to the boil again then reduce the heat to a gentle simmer and cook for 10–12 minutes or until the thickest piece of chicken is cooked through. Remove the chicken from the pan (reserve 1/2 cup of the liquid for the dressing) and cut into bite-sized chunks.

As soon as the rice is cooked, stir in the prepared vegetables (this lightly cooks the vegetables and helps cool the rice). Whisk together the dressing ingredients, then finish the salad by adding the chicken, nuts and dressing to the rice and stirring to combine.

Serve warm, at room temperature, or chilled, garnished with the chopped coriander.

Orzo & Orange Salad with Avocado & Shrimp

At a glance, this may sound like a slightly unorthodox combination, but the colours, textures and, most importantly, the flavours really do work very well together.

This recipe makes a great one dish meal that can be enjoyed immediately, but an additional bonus is that it will also keep for a day or so in the fridge.

For 3–4 servings:
1 cup orzo
1 cup (about 150g) frozen peeled
    prawns or shrimp
2 tablespoons canola or olive oil
2 tablespoons lemon juice
1 teaspoon finely grated lemon rind
1 avocado
2 medium tomatoes
1 orange
2 tablespoons mayonnaise
2 spring onions, thinly sliced
2–3 tablespoons chopped parsley
1/2 teaspoon salt
black pepper to taste

Cook the orzo in plenty of lightly salted, boiling water. When cooked (after about 10 minutes), drain it well and return it to the cooking pot. Add the frozen shrimp or prawns, the oil, lemon juice and finely grated rind and stir to combine.

Leave to stand while you prepare the remaining ingredients. Halve the avocado, remove the stone and peel, then cut the flesh into 1cm cubes. Halve the tomatoes and shake or scoop out (using a teaspoon) the seeds then dice the flesh. Cut the peel and pith from the orange and cut the flesh into 1cm cubes.

Add the avocado, tomatoes and orange to the orzo mixture, along with the remaining ingredients and stir gently to combine. Serve immediately (while still slightly warm), or leave until cooled (or chilled) if you have the time. Add some chunks of crusty bread on the side for an easy meal.

Potato, Bacon & Egg Salad with Toasted Cumin Dressing

I love potato salad! While many people may think of the humble potato salad as a side dish only, I think it warrants consideration as the main part of a meal, especially in this case where the salad is made considerably more substantial with the addition of bacon and eggs.

The dressing is a departure from 'the norm' too, being a lively cumin-flavoured vinaigrette rather than the more traditional mayonnaise-based affair.

For 4 servings:
1kg waxy potatoes
4 large eggs
4 rashers bacon
1–2 teaspoons olive or canola oil
3–4 sticks celery, thinly sliced
1 small red onion, finely diced
2–3 tablespoons chopped coriander or
    parsley

Dressing
2 teaspoons cumin seeds
1/4 cup olive or canola oil
2 tablespoons white wine vinegar
1 tablespoon wholegrain mustard
1/2 teaspoon salt

Scrub the unpeeled potatoes and cut into 2cm chunks or cubes. Place in a large pot, cover with lightly salted water, add the eggs (to hard boil) and boil gently until the potatoes are tender, probably about 12 minutes.

While the potatoes cook, cut the bacon widthwise into 1cm strips. Heat the oil in a large non-stick pan, then add the bacon and fry until lightly browned and crisp. Remove from the pan and drain on paper towels.

Drain the cooked potatoes and eggs, cover with cold water to cool, then drain again. Remove the eggs from their shells and cut each into 4–6 wedges, and place in a large bowl along with celery, onion, bacon and most of the chopped coriander or parsley.

To make the dressing, heat the cumin seeds in a dry pan, shaking frequently to prevent burning, until they smell fragrant. Transfer them to a mortar and pestle and grind well. Combine the ground cumin and remaining dressing ingredients in a small screw topped jar and shake until well combined.

Pour the dressing over the salad, toss gently to combine, then garnish with the remaining herbs and serve.

Crunchy Spinach Salad with Blue Cheese Dressing

I was talking with a group of friends the other day and somehow the subject came around to salads. Interestingly, one of the most popular with the group was also one of the simplest…good old spinach salad, so here it is.

For 3–4 servings:
Dressing
50g blue cheese, crumbled
1 tablespoon wine vinegar
3 tablespoons olive oil
1 tablespoon finely chopped fresh
    chives
2–4 tablespoons milk
salt and pepper to taste

Croutons
4 slices toast sliced bread
2 tablespoons olive or canola oil
garlic salt (optional)

200–250g bacon
300–400g young spinach leaves

To make the dressing, combine the first four ingredients in a blender or food processor. Process until smooth, stopping once or twice to scrape down the sides. Add enough milk to thin the dressing to a pouring consistency, then season to taste with salt and pepper.

To make the croutons, cut the bread into very small cubes (you should have about 2 cups) and put these in a large bowl. Drizzle the oil into the bowl while you toss the bread with a fork or your other hand. Leave as is, or sprinkle lightly with the seasoned salt.

Add to a pan and cook over low heat, turning at intervals, for about 10–15 minutes or until golden brown. Or spread on a large shallow dish and bake in a preheated oven at 150°C for about 5 minutes or until golden brown. Or brown under a moderate grill, watching carefully and turning often so they do not brown unevenly. Set aside while you prepare the remaining ingredients.

To prepare the salad, arrange the bacon on a grill rack and cook close to the heat until lightly browned and crisp, about 5 minutes per side. Cut or break widthwise into strips about 2cm wide.

While the bacon cooks, soak the spinach in a sink full of cold water to remove any grit, then shake or spin dry. Remove and discard the stalks and any large tough looking leaves and place the rest in a large salad bowl.

Just before serving, sprinkle in most of the bacon and croutons and toss gently to combine. Sprinkle the remaining bacon and croutons over the top then drizzle the salad with about half of the dressing.

Serve immediately accompanied with crusty garlic bread and a jug of the remaining dressing.

Char-grilled Vegetable & Feta Salad

We recently got together with several other families for a 'byo' barbecue. Instead of more 'traditional' fare, one friend, Mike, produced an interesting array of vegetables which he char-grilled, then used to make a delicious salad.

It was so good it needed to be put on paper – but remember it's a salad and exact quantities and proportions are not critical, let your imagination be your guide!

For 4-6 servings:

1 medium eggplant
2–3 zucchini, green or yellow
1–2 red or yellow capsicums (peppers)
1–2 bunches asparagus (optional)
10–12 spring onions
2–3 large flat (portobello) mushrooms
2 cloves garlic, crushed, peeled and
    chopped
2 tablespoons olive oil
2 tablespoons balsamic vinegar
pinch salt
black pepper to taste

Dressing

2 tablespoons olive oil
1 tablespoon balsamic vinegar
1 teaspoon wholegrain mustard
1/4–1/2 teaspoon salt

4–6 cups mesclun salad mix
100–150g feta cheese, crumbled

Begin by preparing the vegetables. Cut the eggplant into slices 1.5–2cm thick and the zucchini lengthwise into slices about 1cm thick. Core, deseed and quarter the capsicums. Trim any tough ends from the asparagus (if using), and trim the root ends and floppy green tops from the spring onions. Remove any protruding stems from the mushrooms.

To save brushing the vegetables individually with the marinade place them in a large unpunctured plastic bag. Add the garlic, oil, balsamic vinegar, salt and pepper to taste, then gently turn the vegetables in the mixture until they are evenly coated. Set aside to marinate while you preheat the barbecue or ridged hotplate.

Place the vegetables on the barbecue grill (eggplant, zucchini and capsicums first as they are slower cooking) and cook, turning once or twice until softened and lightly browned (probably about 10–15 minutes in total). Remove the vegetables as they are done and set aside to stand until just warm.

Meanwhile, measure the dressing ingredients into a small screw-topped jar and shake to combine.

Cut the warm vegetables into bite-sized pieces. Spread the mesclun salad mix over a large platter then, just before serving, scatter the cooked vegetables evenly over the top and sprinkle with the crumbled feta. Drizzle with the dressing and serve with plenty of crusty bread.

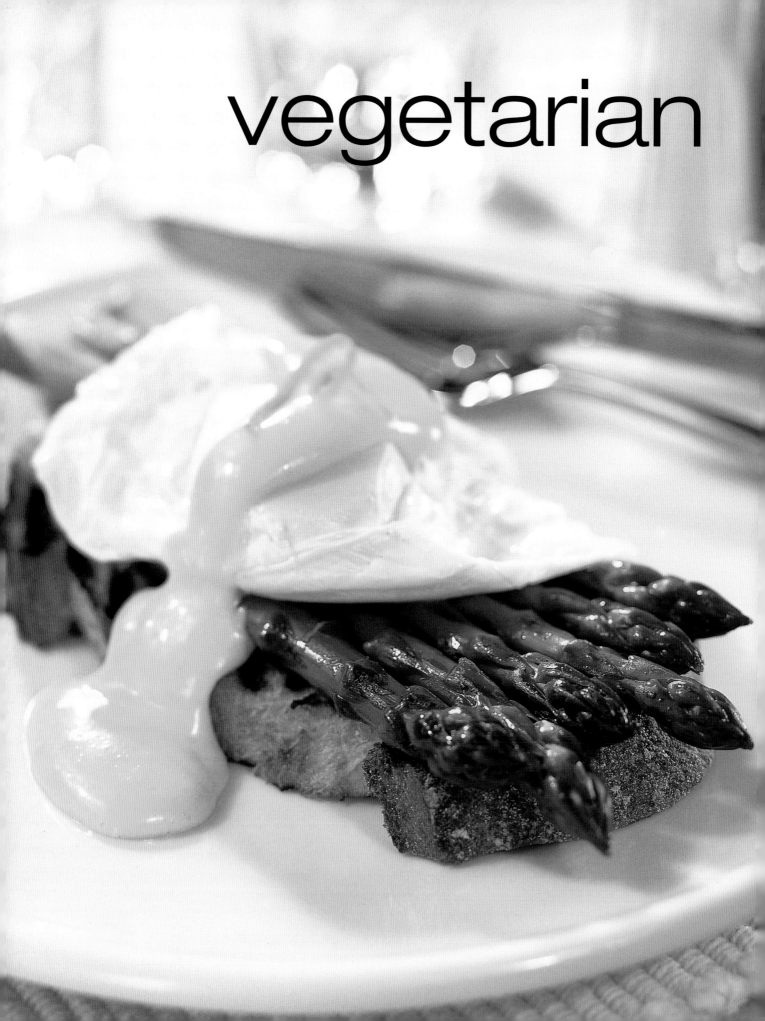

vegetarian

Asparagus with Poached Eggs & Easy Orange Hollandaise Sauce

It easy to subconsciously classify eggs as 'breakfast food' (or perhaps brunch), but there's no need to pigeon-hole them in this way. Who could refuse a meal of poached eggs on top of steaming fresh asparagus, drizzled with hollandaise sauce at any time of the day?

For 3–4 servings:
Easy Orange Hollandaise
2 egg yolks (preferably room temperature)
1 tablespoon each lemon and orange juice
1–2 teaspoons finely grated orange rind
100g butter, cubed
pinch salt (optional)

500–600g asparagus
1–2 tablespoons butter
1 tablespoon white wine or cider vinegar
1/2 teaspoon salt
3–4 eggs
3–4 slices thick toast

Place the egg yolks, lemon juice, orange juice and rind in a food processor (fitted with a metal chopping blade) or blender.

Put the butter in a microwave-safe container, cover to prevent spattering (a saucer works well if your container doesn't have a lid) and microwave on high for 2–3 minutes until bubbling vigorously.

Turn the processor on and add the very hot butter in a thin stream while the motor is running. Season with salt to taste.

The hot butter should thicken the mixture, but if you think the sauce is too runny, transfer back to the microwave container and heat on medium (50%) for 15 seconds then whisk briefly. Repeat if necessary. Warm the same way just before serving.

To cook the asparagus, bring 5–10mm water to a rapid boil in a large (lidded) frypan. Add the asparagus and cook covered for 3–4 minutes, shaking it occasionally. When tender, drain off the water, return it to the hot pan, add the butter and toss to coat evenly. Cover and set aside while you poach the eggs.

Heat about 5cm water in a large pan until it just boils. Add the white wine or cider vinegar and salt and stir. Break the eggs gently into the water. Cook, just at boiling point or slightly below, for about 4–5 minutes or until the yolks are as set as you like.

Place a piece of toast on each plate, divide the asparagus between the plates, arranging it on top of the toast then, using a fish slice or perforated spoon, gently lift an egg onto each pile of asparagus. Pour a little of the warmed sauce over each, serve immediately and enjoy!

Pasta & Tomato Bake

This may not be the most glamorous dish, but it is very tasty and easy to prepare and makes a great meal for a family or hungry flatmates.

Additional bonuses include the fact that most of the ingredients are 'staples' that can be kept on hand in the pantry, and they are economical. Canned tomatoes in juice (either whole or diced) are an incredibly useful item. They can form the basis of anything from soups, to pasta sauces like this, to curries. But the really amazing thing about them is the price – there almost always seems to be one brand or another on sale!

For 4–6 servings:

500g short pasta shapes, eg curls,
    macaroni, spirals or shells
2 medium onions
2 cloves garlic
2 tablespoons canola oil
2 x 400g cans whole or diced
    tomatoes in juice
2–3 tablespoons tomato paste
1 teaspoon salt
1 teaspoon basil
1 teaspoon thyme
black pepper to taste
1–2 cups grated cheese

Cook the pasta in a large pot of lightly salted water and turn the oven on to preheat to 180°C.

While the pasta cooks, dice and sauté the onions and garlic in the oil. When the onion is soft and beginning to turn clear, reduce the heat and add all the remaining ingredients except for the cheese (break up whole tomatoes with the back of a spoon if required). Simmer gently over a low heat for a few minutes until the pasta is cooked.

Drain the cooked pasta, then combine with the tomato mixture in a large shallow casserole or soufflé dish. Sprinkle the cheese evenly over the top. (Although it works just fine with regular 'run of the mill' cheddar, using a cheese like Gruyère – all or even just a proportion – really gives it a lift.)
If you are in a hurry, just brown the top briefly by placing under the grill for a few minutes or if you have time, bake uncovered at 180°C for about 25 minutes or until the top is lightly browned.

Serve with lightly cooked vegetables, a salad and crusty bread if desired.

Variation: *For a fishy alternative, stir in a (drained) 210g can tuna or salmon when you combine the pasta and the sauce. (This is particularly nice if using pasta shells.)*

Rich Mushroom Risotto

If you can find them, and/or bring yourself to part with the cash, a few slices of dried porcini give this risotto a really intense flavour (this is why they are so highly prized). If you don't want to use porcini, you can use dried Chinese (shiitake) mushrooms instead.

For 3–4 servings:

15–20g dried mushrooms (preferably porcini), sliced
1/2 cup hot water
3 tablespoons olive oil
1 medium onion, finely diced
250g Swiss brown mushrooms, sliced
1 cup arborio rice
1 teaspoon dried thyme
black pepper to taste
1/4 cup dry sherry, vermouth or white wine
21/2–3 cups hot water plus
    2 teaspoons instant mushroom stock
3–4 tablespoons freshly grated parmesan (optional)
salt and pepper to taste

Place the dried mushrooms in a shallow container and cover with the hot water. Leave to soak for 15–20 minutes while you prepare the remaining ingredients.

Heat the oil in a large, preferably non-stick pan then add the diced onion. Cook, stirring frequently, until the onion has softened and is turning clear. While the onion cooks, drain the soaked mushrooms, reserving the soaking liquid, and chop into smaller pieces. Add the soaked mushrooms and the fresh mushrooms to the pan and cook, stirring occasionally, until the fresh mushrooms have wilted. Add the rice, thyme and a generous grind of black pepper and stir until the rice is coated with oil.

Reduce the heat a little and pour in the reserved mushroom soaking liquid and the sherry, vermouth or wine and stir continuously until the liquid has almost disappeared. Stir in 1–1 1/2 cups of hot water (plus the instant stock powder) and simmer, stirring frequently, until this has almost disappeared then stir in another cup of water. Continue to cook, stirring frequently, until this too has almost been absorbed. When the rice has cooked for about 20 minutes, try a few grains to see if they are tender right through, if they are still hard in the middle, add another 1/2 cup of water and cook for another 3–4 minutes. Repeat if required. When the risotto is cooked the rice should be coated with a creamy, but not soupy, mixture. If you think it looks too dry add a little extra water.

Stir in the grated parmesan (if using) and season with salt and pepper, if required. Spoon onto plates or bowls and garnish with a few sprigs of thyme, some shaved parmesan and/or strips of grilled mushroom (see below), then serve immediately accompanied with a simple green salad and crusty bread.

Grilled Portobellos

2 tablespoons olive oil • 2 tablespoons balsamic vinegar • 1 tablespoon pesto • 1–2 cloves finely chopped garlic • 4 large portobello mushrooms

Combine the first 4 ingredients in a small bowl.

Brush the top and bottom of the mushrooms with the oil mixture, then arrange them stem side up on a baking tray. Place 5–10cm below a preheated grill and cook for 4–5 minutes. Slice the grilled mushrooms into 1–2cm strips and pile on top of the risotto or serve the risotto piled into the whole mushrooms.

Peppery Chickpea & Potato Curry

Black pepper gives this easy curry an interesting 'kick', quite different from chilli (it seems to hit a different part of the tongue), and without being too hot. I actually like to use a mild curry powder, which gives flavour, without masking the pepper effect.

For 2–3 servings:
1 teaspoon black peppercorns
2 large cloves garlic, peeled
1 whole coriander plant (root and all)
2 tablespoons canola oil
1 tablespoon curry powder
2 medium potatoes, scrubbed and
　　diced
300g can chickpeas, rinsed and
　　drained
2 medium tomatoes, diced
3/4 cup coconut cream
1/2 cup hot water
1 tablespoon soy sauce
1/2 teaspoon sugar
salt to taste
1–2 tablespoons chopped coriander

Measure the peppercorns into a blender or mortar and pestle. Add the garlic and the whole (well washed) coriander plant and blend or pound to a paste. Add the oil and mix well.

Transfer the paste to a medium non-stick pan and cook over a medium heat, stirring frequently, for 2–3 minutes or until fragrant. Stir in the curry powder and cook for 1–2 minutes longer.

Add the potatoes, chickpeas and the tomatoes. Stir so the potatoes are coated with the spice mixture, then add the coconut cream, water, soy sauce and sugar. Bring to the boil, then reduce the heat to a gentle simmer and cook, stirring occasionally, for 10–15 minutes or until the potato cubes are cooked through.

Season to taste with salt, garnish with the chopped coriander and serve. Wilted Cucumber Salad (see below) and naan or roti make great accompaniments.

Wilted Cucumber Salad

1/2 medium telegraph (thin skinned seedless) cucumber • 1 teaspoon salt • 1 cup water • 1 tablespoon white wine vinegar • 1/2–1 teaspoon sesame oil • salt and pepper to taste

Cut the cucumber in half lengthwise, then use a teaspoon to scoop out and discard the seeds. Lie the halves skin-side up on a board and cut into 3mm slices (somehow it always looks a little more exotic if you cut them on a diagonal).

Place the slices in a bowl, sprinkle with the salt then pour in the water and stir. Leave to stand for about 10 minutes, then drain off the brine, rinse the cucumber with fresh water, then pat the slices dry with a clean tea towel.

Transfer the slices back to the bowl, add the vinegar and sesame oil. Toss the cucumber to coat it with the dressing, then season to taste with salt and pepper. Serve immediately or refrigerate until required.

Pappardelle with Blue Cheese & Pecans

If you have a food processor to mix the dough, making fresh pasta at home can be a rewarding experience that need not take all day (it really is different from even bought 'fresh' pasta). If you have a pasta machine, even better, but if you don't it can be rolled with nothing more complicated than a rolling pin. Pappardelle is a pasta shape ideally suited to hand cutting. It is just broad ribbons so there is little messing about once the dough is rolled.

If you don't fancy making your own pasta, you can serve the same sauce with 400g store-bought fresh fettuccine.

For 3–4 servings:

Pasta
2½ cups plain flour
½ teaspoon salt
3 large (60–65g each) eggs
additional flour or water if required

Sauce
3 tablespoons olive oil
1 medium onion
½–¾ cup pecans or walnuts
about 100g spinach leaves, washed
¼ cup cream
½ teaspoon salt
50g blue cheese, cubed or crumbled

To make the pasta, measure the flour and salt into a food processor fitted with a metal chopping blade. With the motor running, add the eggs one at a time. After the last egg is added, the dough should look like crumbs for a few seconds, then form a ball. If the dough has not formed a ball, gradually add a little water (teaspoon by teaspoon) until it does, or if it looks too sticky, add 1–2 tablespoons additional flour.

Tip the dough out onto a lightly floured bench, knead for a couple of minutes, then cover and leave it to stand for 10–15 minutes before rolling. Cut the dough into two or three pieces, leave one out to work with and cover the others. Working on a lightly floured surface (use only just enough flour to prevent sticking at all stages), begin to roll the dough into a thin sheet, turning and rotating it frequently. (Using a pasta machine makes this much faster if you have one.)

When it seems the sheet won't stretch any more, set it aside and move on to the next piece, then return to it later. (This lets the dough sheets 'relax', making them easier to roll out.)

Continue to roll the sheets until each is about 2–3mm thick (don't stop too soon, they will swell quite a lot during cooking), then set them aside for a few minutes before cutting. To cut long pasta, loosely roll up each sheet (square up edges first if you like) and working with a sharp knife, cut the roll (crosswise) into slices of the desired width – 1½–2cm for pappardelle. Each slice should then unroll to make a long ribbon.

To make the sauce, heat 1 tablespoon of the oil in a medium frypan. Add the onion and cook, stirring frequently to prevent browning, for about 5 minutes, or until the onion is soft and clear looking. Stir in the pecans or walnuts and cook for 1–2 minutes longer, then add the spinach. Cover the pan and cook until the spinach wilts, then add the cream and salt. Allow the sauce to come to the boil, then stir in the blue cheese. Remove the sauce from the heat.

Bring a large pot of lightly salted water to a rapid boil. Add the pasta and cook uncovered for 3–5 minutes (depending on how thin you rolled the pasta). Drain the cooked pasta, then return it to the cooking pot. Pour in the remaining 2 tablespoons of oil and toss, then add the sauce and stir gently until it is evenly distributed through the pasta.

Serve immediately with some crusty bread and a tomato salad.

Goat's Cheese & Olive Galette

A galette is somewhere between a freeform (no tin) pie and a pizza – the pastry is rolled out to be bigger than required, the filling is spread over the top then the excess pastry is folded back over the filling, so it is part open and part closed.

This version is particularly close to my heart, because the delicious, surprisingly flaky pastry is a variation of my grandmother's recipe. If you don't want to make the pastry yourself, use 400–500g store-bought savoury short pastry instead.

For 3–4 servings:

Pastry
1½ cups flour
½ teaspoon baking powder
100g cold butter
½ cup cold milk
1 teaspoon white wine vinegar

Filling
2 tablespoons olive or canola oil
2 medium onions, peeled, halved and
  sliced
1 medium red capsicum (pepper),
  cored and sliced
2 medium tomatoes, cubed
1 teaspoon dried thyme
salt and pepper to taste
about 12 olives
50–100g goat's cheese (feta or
  chèvre)

To make the pastry, measure the flour and baking powder into a food processor fitted with a metal chopping blade. Cut the cold butter into 9 cubes and add to the flour. Process in short bursts until the butter is cut into pieces about 5mm across.

Mix the milk and vinegar, then processing in brief pulses slowly pour in just enough liquid to make the pastry mixture look like bread crumbs that will just form a ball when gently squeezed (stop frequently to test this).

Press the dough into a ball, flatten this into a disk, wrap loosely and refrigerate while you make the filling.

Preheat the oven to 180°C. Heat the oil in a large frypan. Add the onion and cook over a medium-high heat, stirring occasionally, for 3–4 minutes until the onion has softened and is beginning to brown. Stir in the capsicum, tomatoes and thyme and cook for 5–6 minutes longer, stirring frequently until the capsicum is soft and the tomato pieces have lost their shape. Remove from the heat and season to taste with salt and pepper.

Working on a lightly floured surface, roll the pastry out to form a round about 45–50cm across.

Roll the pastry around your rolling pin and lift it onto a teflon or baking paper-lined oven tray. Spread the filling mix over the middle 30cm or so, then sprinkle the filling with the olives and crumbled cheese.

Fold the uncovered pastry edges back over the filling, making five or six tucks around the inner edge so it will sit flat.

Place in the middle of the oven and bake for 15–20 minutes until the pastry is golden brown. Remove from the oven and allow to cool for several minutes before serving with a simple salad on the side.

Pumpkin, Spinach & Feta Cakes

The salty tang of the feta in these delicious cakes goes really well with the sweetness of the pumpkin. The cumin and curry powders give an interesting flavour, suggesting something slightly exotic, but without really dominating.
In fact, I think the flavours are interesting enough that no sauce is required, but if you want you could serve them with yoghurt based raita, sweet chilli sauce, or even tomato sauce on the side.

For 3–4 servings (12 large cakes):
250g peeled and cubed pumpkin
2 large eggs
1/4 cup milk
125g frozen spinach, thawed
100–125g feta cheese, crumbled
1/2 cup self-raising flour
1/2 teaspoon ground cumin
1/2 teaspoon curry powder
1/2 teaspoon salt
black pepper to taste
2–3 tablespoons canola oil for frying

Place the pumpkin in a small bowl or roasting bag and microwave for 4–5 minutes on high (100%), stirring after 2 minutes, or until tender. Mash roughly then set aside.

Break the eggs into a medium-sized bowl, then add the milk, spinach and feta. Add the mashed pumpkin and stir until well mixed. Sprinkle in the flour, cumin, curry powder, salt and pepper to taste and gently fold together, until all ingredients are just combined.

Heat 1 tablespoon of the oil in a large non-stick pan. Drop serving spoon-size blobs of the batter into the pan leaving several centimetres between each to allow easier turning. Cook over a medium heat for 2–3 minutes per side, or until golden brown. Arrange cooked cakes on a double layer of paper towels and keep warm while you cook the remaining batter in batches that fit comfortably in the pan.

Serve with one or two interesting salads and sweet chilli or tomato sauce for dipping if desired.

Alain's Authentic Cheese Fondue

Fondue is a fashion victim! These days it seems the only time you're likely to encounter a cheese fondue is when someone is trying to recreate 70s' kitsch. This is a pity because they are actually a simple and delicious meal to share with family or friends.
My opinion may be coloured by childhood experiences, or fond recollections of the 'real thing' shared in Switzerland a few years ago, but if you haven't tried it, it is definitely worth a go.

For 4 servings:
Sauce
400–450g Gruyère or Emmenthal
   cheese
3 tablespoons flour
1 clove garlic, crushed and peeled
2 cups medium dry white wine
   (Riesling is ideal)
2 tablespoons brandy or vodka
about 1/4 teaspoon grated nutmeg
black pepper to taste

2 loaves good French bread, cut in
   3cm cubes
2–3 tart Braeburn or Granny Smith
   apples, cubed
grapes (optional)
cubed pear (optional)

Grate the cheese (a food processor does this very quickly) then sprinkle it with the flour and toss to combine.

Rub the inside of a fondue or heavy pot with the garlic, then add the wine. Heat until bubbles begin to rise off the bottom, then add the cheese, 1/2 cup by 1/2 cup, stirring constantly until the cheese has melted. Stir in the brandy or vodka and nutmeg, then season to taste with black pepper. Set the pot over its burner or a couple of tea-light candles.

Prepare the remaining ingredients and arrange the cubes of bread, apple, pear and whole grapes around the pot. To eat, spear the cubes or grapes with long-handled fondue forks or bamboo skewers, dunk in the fondue and enjoy!

fish

Fish Tacos

I always thought that a taco was a folded, crisp fried tortilla. A recent trip to the United States has, however, altered this perception – soft, filled tortillas like these were definitely sold as tacos so who am I to argue…Whatever the name, they are delicious and so easy to prepare!

For 2–3 servings:
300–400g firm white fish fillets (like tarakihi, gurnard or snapper)
juice of 1 lime (or 2 tablespoons lemon juice)
1 teaspoon ground cumin

Salsa
2 large ripe tomatoes
1 ripe avocado
1/4 cup chopped coriander
1 finely chopped spring onion
juice 1 lime (or 2 tablespoons lemon juice)
1/2 teaspoon salt
1/2 teaspoon sugar

2–3 teaspoons olive or canola oil
6–10 soft corn tortillas
Tabasco or other chilli sauce to serve (optional)

Arrange the fish fillets in a shallow dish and sprinkle both sides first with the lime (or lemon) juice, then sprinkle lightly with the cumin. Leave to stand while you prepare the salsa.

To make the salsa, halve the tomatoes then scoop out, discard the seeds and cut the flesh into 7mm cubes. Halve and peel the avocado and cut into similar sized cubes. Put the diced tomatoes and avocado in a small bowl, add the remaining salsa ingredients and mix gently to combine.

Heat 2 teaspoons of oil in a large non-stick pan, add the fish fillets and cook for about 2 minutes per side, depending on thickness, until just cooked through, then place in a warmed serving dish.

While the fish cooks, warm the tortillas by either placing the bag in the microwave and heating on high (100%) for about 1 minute or warm each one briefly in a lightly oiled pan or on a hot plate. Wrap in a clean dry tea towel to keep warm.

To assemble, break the fish into 4–5cm chunks, place several chunks on a tortilla, add a generous spoonful of the salsa and roll loosely. Serve with plain or green rice and a simple salad if desired.

Variations: *If you want to make this dish for larger groups, just multiply the quantities given. Instead of pan-frying the fish which is fiddly in bulk, flash bake it in an oven preheated to 225°C for 5–6 minutes. This recipe is also well suited to barbecuing when you feel like something a little different – both the fish and the tortillas can be cooked very successfully on the hot plate.*

Note: *Soft corn tortillas are now available in 'long life' packs in the Mexican foods sections of larger supermarkets – keep a packet in the pantry so they're available when the mood strikes.*

Charmoula Fish Tagine

Olives, lemons and a hint of chilli feature in many Moroccan dishes and this one is no exception. Since all three flavours also work well individually with fish, it's no surprise they all combine well in this delicious tagine.

Charmoula is used here as a marinade for the fish, but it is also often used as a sauce or 'dressing' for pan fried fish fillets, grilled lamb, beef or even chicken – apparently it features very prominently in North African cuisine.

For 4 servings:
600–800g fish
charmoula (see below)
4 medium (about 500g) carrots
2 tablespoons olive oil
1 medium onion, peeled and sliced
2–3 medium tomatoes, sliced
1/2–1 teaspoon salt
black pepper to taste
1 lemon, thinly sliced
1 medium red capsicum (pepper),
    deseeded and cut into 5mm strips
about 20 olives

Preheat the oven to 225°C. While the oven heats cut the fish into even-sized, easily managed chunks and place in a plastic bag or arrange in a shallow tray. Add the charmoula and massage the bag, or turn the fish so it is evenly coated with the sauce, then set it aside to marinate.

Cut the carrots into very fine ribbons using a sharp potato peeler or julienne. Non-stick spray a 20 x 30cm casserole dish, then add the carrot ribbons and 1 tablespoon of the oil and toss gently until they are evenly coated. Sprinkle the onion slices over the carrot, then place the casserole dish in the oven and bake uncovered for 15 minutes.

Remove the casserole from the oven. Arrange the tomato slices in a layer over the onions, spread the fish evenly over the tomatoes, drizzling with any remaining marinade. Cover the fish with a layer of lemon slices, then sprinkle with the capsicum strips and scatter the olives over the top. Drizzle with the remaining oil.

Cover tightly and bake for 15 minutes, then uncover and cook for a further 5 minutes. Serve with couscous and a green or tomato salad.

Charmoula
3 cloves garlic, peeled • 1/4 cup chopped flat leaf parsley • 1/4 cup chopped coriander • minced red or green chilli to taste (try about 1 teaspoon) • 2 teaspoons paprika • juice 1 lemon • 4–6 tablespoons olive oil

Place first six ingredients in a blender or food processor. Process until the herbs are finely chopped then add the oil a little at a time, processing between additions, until you have a pourable sauce.

Almond Crusted Tandoori Salmon

I've seen several recipes for Tandoori-style salmon recently, but I have to confess I had reservations about the curry-salmon combination until I actually tried it for myself.

Indian curry pastes like the one I've used here are now available in most supermarkets. Some brands are labelled by heat (hot, medium or mild) and other brands by style (Vindaloo, Tandoori etc.). I usually buy a medium Tika Masala style which works pretty well in most situations, but you can select any product to suit your own tastes.

Because this salmon is oven-baked it is easy to multiply this simple yet elegant recipe to serve for company.

For 2–3 servings:
1 clove garlic, peeled
1 teaspoon grated ginger
1 tablespoon medium curry paste
1 tablespoon lemon juice
1/2 teaspoon salt
1/2 cup natural unsweetened yoghurt
2–3 (about 150g each) pieces salmon
    fillet, pin boned
3–4 tablespoons flaked or sliced
    almonds

Put the first six ingredients in a blender or food processor and process the marinade until smooth. Place the salmon fillets in a plastic bag, pour in the marinade and massage so the fish is evenly covered. Leave to stand for 15–20 minutes while the oven heats to 200°C.

Remove the salmon from the marinade and place, skin side down, on a non-stick sprayed metal baking tray (I use a sponge roll tin). Pour about a tablespoon of the marinade over each piece and then sprinkle them liberally with sliced almonds.

Bake for 10–12 minutes until the salmon is just cooked through at the thickest part (test by piercing a piece with a sharp knife and looking in), and the almonds are lightly browned.

Serve with Lemon Rice (see below) or plain rice and a simple green salad.

Note: *Salmon fillets have a row of fine 'pin' bones running more or less down the centre, it is always more pleasant to eat if these are removed. Some good shops do this as a matter of course, others will on request, or you can do it yourself at home. Lie the fillet skin side down on the bench run your fingers up the fillet (from the tail to head end) and you will feel where they are – simply grab the end with tweezers or pliers and pull them out.*

Lemon Rice

1 cup basmati rice • 1/8 teaspoon turmeric • 1/2 teaspoon salt • finely grated zest of 1 lemon • 2 cups boiling water • 3 tablespoons canola oil • 1/4 cup cashew nuts, roughly chopped • 1 teaspoon mustard seeds • 1/2 teaspoon cumin seeds (optional) • 8–10 curry leaves • juice of 1/2 lemon

Measure the rice, turmeric, salt, lemon zest and water into a microwave bowl. Cover and microwave for 15 minutes on medium (50%).

When the rice is cooked, heat the oil in a large non-stick pan. Add the cashews, mustard and cumin seeds (if using) and cook for 1–2 minutes. Drop in the curry leaves and sizzle briefly, then add the cooked rice and lemon juice. Toss to combine and transfer to a serving dish.

Serve as an interesting alternative to plain rice with most curries.

Foil Wrapped Fish

Being an island nation full of fisher-persons (or budding fisher-persons), it is often handy to know a no-fuss way to deal with whole fish. 'Foil wrapping' is a great example, especially as it is so versatile.

It can be used with almost any type of fish (including trout) and you can vary the flavourings depending what you have on hand – the only essentials are the fish and the foil – a lemon or two is a real bonus, but they can be omitted at a pinch. The heat source can vary too – the barbecue or oven both work just fine. Here are two possible variants on the theme, one fairly traditional and the other with a more Pacific-Asian flavour. Both are for a fish of about 1kg (cleaned), but exact quantities are not critical.

For 2–3 servings:
1 whole (about 1kg) fish

Seasoning 1
1 teaspoon paprika
1 teaspoon garlic salt
1 teaspoon celery salt (optional)
1 teaspoon dill leaf
about 1/4 teaspoon thyme
black pepper to taste
several sprigs fresh herbs (optional)
or
Seasoning 2
1/2 cup coconut cream
1–2 cloves garlic, peeled and chopped
1 tablespoon finely chopped ginger
2 tablespoons soy sauce
1/2 teaspoon chilli powder
juice of 1 lemon

1 lemon (optional)
salt and pepper to taste

Make 2–3 deep slashes on both sides of the fish (this helps even cooking). Unless you want to eat the skin, the (cleaned) fish can even be cooked unscaled as the skin lifts off easily once the fish is cooked. Lay out a double layer of foil, big enough to wrap the fish (wider foil is a real help here).

Combine the seasoning ingredients (using either Seasoning 1 or Seasoning 2) and sprinkle about a third of the mixture over the foil where the fish will lie. Place the fish on top, rub or sprinkle a little of the seasoning mixture into the cavity, then sprinkle the remainder over the upper side. If you have a lemon handy, slice it thinly and place a couple of slices on either side of the fish, and stuff the rest into the cavity (add the optional fresh herbs in Seasoning 1 in the same way).

Carefully fold up and seal the foil package, trying to make sure there is no air around the fish. Place the package on the barbecue or fire and cook, turning over every five minutes. (If using an oven, bake at 180°C for 12–15 minutes per 500g fish.) The only way to know if the fish is cooked is to open the package every now and then and check it – when the flesh at the thickest part will flake the fish is cooked. When the fish is cooked, remove it from the heat and leave to stand for about 10 minutes, or until cool enough to handle.

Discard the head, tail and fins, then peel away the skin. Lift the flesh off the bones and place on clean foil or in a bowl and sprinkle with the cooking juices. Taste and season with salt and pepper if required.

Serve as is with rice, crusty bread or potatoes and a salad.

Variation: *I like to use fish fillets (monkfish or snapper) and Seasoning 2 to make individual serving-sized packages. Allow 150–200g fish fillets per person and wrap in smaller squares of foil or use squares of banana leaf (look in the frozen food section of Asian-food stores) sealed with a toothpick. Cook as above but reduce the time to about 8–10 minutes.*

Tips for cleaning fish: *My first piece of advice on cleaning fish is to get someone else to do it for you! Sadly, this is not always possible and in this case, proceed as follows: Using a sharp knife cut from the 'throat' up to the back of the head, then, starting from the tail, slit up the belly to the head, then gently remove and discard the guts and gills. Rinse inside and out with fresh water or sea water.*

Greek-style Baked Fish with Garlic & Lemon Potatoes

It's amazing how the flavours and aromas of food can bring the memories flooding back. Whenever I make these potatoes I can picture vividly the beach in Greece where I first tried them.

Because the fish cooks so quickly in the hot oven, it actually pays to start the potatoes first so everything is ready at the same time.

For 3–4 servings:

1kg potatoes
2 cloves garlic, crushed, peeled and
  chopped
1/2 cup chicken stock
1–2 tablespoons lemon juice
3 tablespoons olive oil
salt and pepper to taste
1 medium onion, quartered, peeled
  and sliced
400g can whole or diced tomatoes in
  juice
about 700g white fish fillets (tarakihi,
  gurnard etc.)
finely grated zest and juice of 1 lemon
1/2 teaspoon salt
2–3 slices stale bread
1 clove garlic, peeled
handful parsley
1–2 tablespoons olive oil

Preheat the oven to 225°C. Scrub the potatoes and cut into 2cm cubes. Non-stick spray a shallow 20 x 30cm casserole dish. Add the potatoes, garlic, stock, lemon juice and 2 tablespoons of the oil, then toss gently to combine. Season to taste with the salt and pepper, then place in the middle of the heated oven and cook for 20–25 minutes until golden brown, turning them gently after about 10 minutes (or when you add the fish).

Once the potatoes are in the oven, heat the remaining tablespoon of oil in a medium frypan. Add the onion and sauté until soft, then stir in the tomatoes, breaking up the whole tomatoes with a spoon if required. Allow the tomato mixture to come to the boil, then remove from the heat.

Non-stick spray another 20 x 30cm casserole dish and pour in the tomato mixture. Arrange the fish fillets on top of the tomatoes and sprinkle them evenly with the lemon zest and juice and salt.

Tear each slice of bread into 4–6 pieces, then place in a blender or food processor with the garlic and a good handful of parsley. Process until the bread is crumbed, then with the blender/processor running drizzle in enough oil to make the crumbs look moist. Sprinkle the crumbs over the fish.

When the potatoes have cooked for about 10 minutes, slide the casserole of fish in alongside, or place on the rack above if there isn't space (stir the potatoes at this stage if you haven't already) and cook for 12 minutes until the crumbs are golden brown.

Allow the fish to stand for a few minutes, then serve with the potatoes and Easy Tomato & Cucumber Salad (see below).

Easy Tomato & Cucumber Salad

Allow about one medium-sized ripe tomato and about 5cm cucumber per person. Cut the tomatoes and cucumber into 1 1/2–2cm cubes. Place in a bowl and sprinkle with about 1/2 teaspoon balsamic vinegar and 1 teaspoon extra virgin olive oil per serving. Add a handful of olives (optional), a few chopped or torn basil leaves, toss and then season to taste with salt and pepper.

Paprika 'Smoked' Fish on Fruity Couscous

Smoked paprika has an amazing colour, flavour and aroma. It gives other foods a distinctly 'smoked' flavour, without the need for using an actual smoker. Although it is relatively expensive, and you'll probably have to look in a speciality food store or delicatessen to find it, this Spanish gem is definitely worth having on hand. The good news is that a little goes a long way, and a small tin will keep almost indefinitely in the fridge.

As the fish actually cooks so fast, the best way to attack this dish is to coat the fish with the seasoned flour then leave it to stand while you prepare the Fruity Couscous and Smoky Coriander Mayonnaise, then fry the fish at the last minute.

For 3–4 servings:
3 tablespoons flour
2 teaspoons smoked paprika
1 teaspoon garlic salt
black pepper to taste
600–800g white fish fillets (tarakihi,
    snapper, gurnard or blue cod)
1 tablespoon olive or canola oil

Measure the first four ingredients into a large plastic bag. Cut the fish fillets into even-sized pieces, so there will be two or three pieces per serving.

Drop two pieces into the flour mixture and shake the bag so the fish is evenly coated. Remove the fish pieces from the flour, shaking off the excess, and lie it on a board or rack. Repeat this process until all the fish is flour coated. Leave to stand while you prepare the Fruity Couscous and mayonnaise.

To cook, heat the oil in a large non-stick pan. Add the fish pieces and cook over a medium-high heat for 2–3 minutes (this will depend on the thickness of the fish) or until golden brown, then turn the fish and repeat for the other side.

Serve the fish on or alongside a generous spoonful of Fruity Couscous topped with a dollop of Smoky Coriander Mayonnaise. A simple green salad makes an ideal accompaniment.

Fruity Couscous

1 cup couscous • 1 cup boiling chicken stock (or 1 cup boiling water plus 1 teaspoon instant stock powder) • 1 tablespoon olive or canola oil • 1/4 cup slivered almonds • 1/4 cup chopped dried apricots • 1/4 cup currants • 1–2 tablespoons lemon juice • 1 tablespoon olive oil • 2–3 tablespoons each chopped parsley and coriander • 1/2 teaspoon salt

Put the couscous in a large bowl, add the boiling stock and leave to stand for about 5 minutes. Meanwhile, heat the oil in a large pan (you can use this for the fish later). Add the almonds and cook, stirring frequently, until they just begin to colour, then stir in the chopped apricots and the currants. Cook for 1–2 minutes longer until the currants puff up, stirring continuously, then remove from the pan.

Add the fruit and nuts to the couscous, stir with a fork to 'fluff' the couscous up, then add the lemon juice, second measure of oil, herbs and salt, then mix again. Taste and add a little more salt if required.

Smoky Coriander Mayonnaise

1 large egg • 1 clove garlic, peeled • 1 tablespoon lemon juice • 1 teaspoon Dijon mustard • 1 teaspoon salt • 1 teaspoon smoked paprika • 3/4 cup canola oil • about 1/4 cup olive oil • 1–2 tablespoons roughly chopped coriander

Break the egg into a blender or food processor. Add the garlic, lemon juice, mustard, salt and paprika. Process to combine, then with the motor running, add the oil in a thin stream, until the mayonnaise is thick enough to hold its shape when the motor is stopped (you may not require all the oil). Add the coriander and process again until evenly distributed.

Use immediately or transfer to a clean airtight container and store in the fridge for up to one week.

Note: *For 'plain' mayonnaise simply omit the paprika and coriander.*

Mussels in Red Curry Sauce

Fresh (live) mussels must be about the best value seafood around. Better still, as well as being delicious, they also have high levels of all sorts of vitamins and minerals, including iron, and like most seafood, are low in fat.

For 2–3 servings:

1kg live mussels
1 tablespoon canola oil
1 small onion
2 cloves garlic, crushed, peeled and
   chopped
1cm piece fresh ginger, peeled and
   chopped
1 medium carrot, finely diced
1 red capsicum (pepper), finely diced
1 tablespoon red curry paste
4 kaffir lime leaves
1 stalk lemongrass, bruised
3/4 cup coconut cream
2 tablespoons fish sauce
1/2 teaspoon each sugar and salt
chopped coriander to garnish

Pull the beards (any hairy looking bits) from the mussels, then set them aside. Heat the oil in a large pot that has a tight fitting lid (you need a lid to steam the mussels open). Add the onion and garlic and cook, stirring frequently, until the onion is soft, then add the ginger, carrot and capsicum. Continue to cook until the capsicum has softened, then add the curry paste and cook, stirring continuously, for 1–2 minutes longer.

Stir in the lime leaves, lemongrass and coconut cream. Bring the mixture to a rapid boil and add the mussels. Cover and cook for about 5–6 minutes, stirring once or twice.

Stir in the fish sauce, sugar and salt. Divide the mussels between bowls, discarding any that have not opened, then divide the sauce evenly between the bowls too.

Garnish with chopped coriander and serve immediately, with steamed rice or crusty bread to mop up the sauce on the side.

Steamer Basket Fish

This is a simple but delicious recipe. I like to cook and serve it in individual bamboo steamer baskets, I have three or four that are about 15cm across which are perfect. Look for them in stores selling Asian foods and supplies, they are inexpensive and good to have on hand.

For 2 servings:

100g rice sticks
1 medium carrot, finely julienned
1/2 sheet nori, thinly sliced
about 300g thinnish white fish fillets
   (tarakihi or gurnard)
2 thin slices ginger, julienned
2 teaspoons sesame oil
2 teaspoons light soy sauce

Place the rice sticks in a large bowl and cover them with boiling water. Leave them to soak for 5 minutes or until they are soft through, then drain.

Divide the noodles between two steamer baskets. Top the noodles with the carrot and scatter with two-thirds of the nori. Lay the fish fillets across the bed of carrots and noodles (I like to use thinnish fillets so they cook faster). Sprinkle the fillets with the ginger, sesame oil and soy sauce, finish by adding the remaining strips of nori.

Stack the baskets and cover the upper one with a close fitting lid. Half fill a small pot (that you can snugly rest the baskets over) with hot water and bring it to a rapid boil. (I don't like to stack the baskets more than two high – I don't think the top ones get as hot. If you want to do more baskets, steam them over more pots.) Place the steamer baskets on top of the pot, and cook for 4 minutes before swapping the top one for the bottom one. Replace the basket and steam for 3–5 minutes longer until the fish is just cooked (poke it with a sharp knife at the thickest point and see if it is opaque in the middle).

Remove the lid, place the baskets on flat plates and serve. Bok choy or choy sum steamed in another basket, and drizzled with a little soy sauce and sesame oil makes a great accompaniment.

Fish Tika Masala

I came up with this recipe to try to emulate the flavours of fish curries I've enjoyed in restaurants. For authenticity I have used a two-step cooking process – grilling the marinated fish, then adding it to a simmering sauce. This gives an excellent result. However, the sauce is very good in its own right and on occasions I have been known to skip the marinating and grilling and add the fish directly to the sauce, simmering it for a few minutes longer until it is cooked through. Quicker, easier and still very good!

For 4 servings:

500–600g fairly firm white fish fillets (tarakihi, snapper, monkfish, warehou etc.)

1/4 cup plain unsweetened yoghurt

1 tablespoon honey

1 tablespoon lemon juice

1 clove garlic, crushed, peeled and chopped

1/2 teaspoon turmeric

1 teaspoon each cumin, coriander and fenugreek seeds

400g can whole or diced tomatoes in juice

1/2–3/4 cup cream

2 tablespoons grated ginger

1 tablespoon each tomato paste and honey

1/2 teaspoon chilli powder

1 teaspoon salt

1 teaspoon garam masala

2–3 tablespoons chopped coriander

Cut the fish into cubes or chunks 2–3cm thick, then put in a plastic bag with the yoghurt, honey, lemon juice, garlic and turmeric. Massage bag to mix the fish and marinade, then set aside for 15 minutes or refrigerate for longer.

To make the sauce, place the whole spices in a large dry pan and heat until they smell toasted and fragrant. Transfer to a blender and grind, then add the next six ingredients and whiz again until smooth. Pour the mixture into the pan and heat to boiling, then reduce the heat and leave to simmer gently for 5–10 minutes, stirring occasionally.

Heat the grill and arrange the fish on a lightly oiled, foil-covered metal tray. Grill the fish 5cm from the heat for 5 minutes or until just cooked. Meanwhile add the garam masala and coriander to the sauce and stir, then gently add the grilled fish and simmer for 2–3 minutes longer. Serve over steamed rice and accompany with naan or other Indian breads.

Variation: *For Chicken Tika Masala simply replace the fish with thin strips of skinless, boneless chicken breast or tenderloins.*

Fish Fillets in Creamy Curry Sauce

Maybe it's something to do with our Pacific Rim location or perhaps it's just because they really do just belong together, but I love the combination of fish and coconut cream.

In this simple recipe, firm fish fillets are lightly fried then simmered briefly in a delicious coconut cream based curry sauce.

For 3–4 servings:
1 medium onion, peeled
2 cloves garlic, peeled
1 tablespoon chopped ginger
1 x 10cm red chilli, deseeded
1 teaspoon turmeric
1 teaspoon ground cumin
1 teaspoon coriander
1/2 teaspoon ground fenugreek
400–500g firm fish fillets
1–2 tablespoons flour
2 tablespoons canola or other oil
3/4 cup coconut cream
1/2 cup hot water
2 tablespoons fish sauce
chopped fresh coriander and chilli
    slices (optional) to garnish

Blend or process the first eight ingredients to a smooth paste, then leave to stand for a few minutes while you prepare the fish.

Cut the fillets into even-sized pieces, so there will be 3–4 largish chunks per serving. Lightly dust both sides of the fish with flour while 1 tablespoon of the oil heats in a large non-stick pan.

Arrange the fish in the pan and cook for about 2 minutes per side until lightly browned and barely cooked through, then remove from the pan.

Add the remaining oil to the pan, then stir in the spice paste. Cook for 2–3 minutes, stirring continuously, then pour in the coconut cream, water and fish sauce. Stir to mix, bring to the boil, then reduce the heat to a gentle simmer and cook for about 5 minutes before adding back the fish pieces.

Gently turn the fish once so it is coated with the sauce, garnish with chopped coriander and chilli (if using) and serve immediately once the fish has heated through.

Plain rice, lightly cooked bok choy or broccolini and naan bread or roti make ideal accompaniments.

Za'atar Crusted Tuna Steaks

Za'atar is a seasoning mix of North African or Middle Eastern origin – it is a fragrant blend of toasted sesame seeds, thyme and sumac (a fruity but tangy spice). For good measure I like to throw a little garlic into the mix as well. I first came across this recipe looking for a way to use sumac, which I had heard of but didn't really know how to use. Having just 'discovered' it relatively recently it seems to be popping up all over the place – on menus, pre-made in stores etc.

In addition to using za'atar as a seasoning for fish, chicken or lamb, it can be used for dipping oil-moistened bread like dukkah (a spice and nut blend), or even stirred into thick creamy yoghurt for an easy dip.

For 4 servings:
Za'atar
2 tablespoons sesame seeds
2 tablespoons sumac
2 tablespoons fresh thyme
2 cloves garlic, peeled
1/2–1 teaspoon salt

4 x 2–3cm thick tuna steaks (each about 150g)
2–3 teaspoons olive oil

Measure the sesame seeds into a medium pot or frypan. Heat over a moderate heat, shaking the pan frequently until the seeds turn from pale to golden brown. Tip the seeds from the pan into a blender or spice grinder. Add the sumac, thyme, garlic and salt and blend until finely chopped and uniform.

Sprinkle the za'atar into a shallow bowl or plate. Gently press both sides of the tuna steaks into the mixture, then leave them to stand for about 5 minutes.

Heat 2 teaspoons of the oil in a non-stick pan. Add the tuna and cook for 1–2 minutes per side depending on the thickness and how well you like tuna cooked (I like it pink in the middle so usually opt for about 1 1/2 minutes per side). Add the extra oil for the second side if the pan is looking dry.

Serve immediately accompanied with plain or Fruity Couscous (see page 56) and Easy Tomato & Cucumber Salad (see page 55).

Green Sauced Grilled Fish

I guess this sauce, or in this case marinade, is really a very simple version of charmoula (which I can never pronounce, or spell). It could be called parsley sauce, but somehow green sauce sounds more mysterious and interesting – like the resulting fish.

For 2–3 servings:
400–500g white fish fillets (tarakihi or snapper)
1 clove garlic
1/2 cup roughly chopped parsley
1 tablespoon chilli oil
1 tablespoon olive oil
1 tablespoon lemon juice
1/2 teaspoon salt

Arrange the fish on a double layer of foil. Place remaining ingredients in a food processor or blender and process to form a smoothish paste. Spread the sauce paste over the fish and leave to stand for five minutes or longer (refrigerate for several hours if desired).

Turn your grill on to its highest heat and place a solid tray (I use a sponge roll tin) 5–7cm below the heat. When the grill has heated, carefully slide the fish, still on the foil, onto the hot tray (this will help cook the bottom of the fish so you don't need to turn it). Cook for 3–5 minutes, depending on the thickness of the fish, until the fish has just changed from translucent to opaque white at the thickest part.

Remove from the heat and serve immediately. A few wedges of lemon, crusty bread or rolls and a big green salad or coleslaw make ideal accompaniments.

Lemony Salmon Risotto

When it occurred to me that I could make a fish-based risotto using cubes of salmon fillet, with its beautiful colour and texture, the idea began to have a much greater appeal than it had when contemplating the 'white on white' of 'conventional' fish with rice. I still like to keep the rice as pale as possible but love the contrast once the salmon, prawns and peas are added at the end.

For 2–3 servings:
2 tablespoons olive oil
1 medium onion, peeled and finely diced
2 cloves garlic, crushed, peeled and chopped
1 cup arborio rice
3 cups chicken stock, warmed
zest 1 lemon
1/2–1 cup hot water
1/4 cup dry sherry
1/2–1 teaspoon salt
200–300g salmon fillet, skinned and cut in 1cm cubes
1/2–1 cup cooked peeled prawns (optional)
1/2 cup frozen peas
1/4 cup grated parmesan
1–2 tablespoons chopped basil (optional)

Heat the oil in a large pan. Add the onion and garlic and cook for about 5 minutes, stirring frequently to prevent any browning until the onion is soft. Tip the rice into the pan and stir until the grains are coated with oil, continue to cook, stirring frequently, until the rice begins to look milky white, about 2–3 minutes.

Pour in half the warmed stock and cook over a medium heat, stirring continuously until this has almost all been absorbed, then add the remaining stock and the lemon zest. Continue to cook, stirring occasionally, until this too has almost been absorbed (by this time the rice should have been cooking for about 15 minutes). Begin testing the rice, if it is not tender through and is looking dry, add 1/2 a cup of water and cook for a few minutes longer then test again and repeat if necessary.

As soon as the rice is tender through, add the sherry, salt, cubed salmon, prawns and peas. Stir gently and cook for 3–4 minutes longer until the salmon is just cooked through, then stir in the parmesan.
Serve garnished with some chopped basil and a green salad on the side.

Pasta with Smoked Fish & Olives

A crunchy breadcrumb mixture makes this simple pasta dish interesting and a little different.

For 2–3 servings:
250g long pasta (spaghetti, fettuccine etc.)
2–3 slices (about 75g) stale bread
2 tablespoons olive oil
1 clove garlic, peeled and chopped
2 tablespoons pinenuts (optional)
2 tablespoons chopped parsley
150–250g skinless, boneless, hot smoked fish fillets
1–2 tablespoons extra virgin olive oil
1/4–1/2 cup kalamata olives
1/4 cup sliced char-grilled red pepper (optional)
juice 1/2 lemon
salt and pepper to taste

Put the pasta on to cook in plenty of lightly salted boiling water. While the pasta cooks food process or grate the bread into coarse crumbs. Heat the first measure of oil in a large pan over a medium heat, then stir in the crumbs, garlic, pinenuts (if using) and parsley. Cook, stirring frequently, until the crumbs are golden brown (about 5 minutes), then remove from the heat. Flake or break the smoked fish into bite-sized pieces.

When the pasta is cooked, drain it then return it to the cooking pot. Add the fish, the second measure of oil, olives, peppers (if using), lemon juice, salt and pepper to taste, then toss to mix.

Arrange the pasta on plates or a platter and top with the crumb mixture. Serve with a salad for a simple summer meal.

chicken

Lemongrass Curried Chicken

This is a great recipe if you're expecting company for dinner. Not only is it delicious and sure to generate compliments, but after a little initial preparation (which can actually be done well ahead of time) you just sling it in the oven for 40 minutes. This leaves you free to socialise rather than stuck slaving over a hot stove as your guests arrive.

For 6–8 servings:

3 stems lemongrass
2 large cloves garlic, peeled
2½cm piece ginger, peeled
1 medium onion, peeled and roughly
  chopped
1 tablespoon minced red chilli
1 tablespoon fish sauce
1 teaspoon turmeric
400g can coconut cream
8 large chicken thighs
2 tablespoons canola or other oil
½ cup boiling water
4 kaffir lime leaves
2 stems lemongrass, halved
  lengthways
2 tablespoons dark soy sauce
2 tablespoons brown sugar

Peel any tough outer leaves from the outside of the lemongrass stalks and roughly chop the tender whitish parts. Add these to a blender or food processor with the next six ingredients and blend or process until finely chopped. Pour in ¼ cup of the coconut cream and process again to make a smooth paste.

Trim any obvious excess flaps of skin and fat from the chicken while the oil heats in a large non-stick pan. Working in two batches, lightly brown the chicken on both sides (3–4 minutes per side). Remove the browned chicken from the pan and drain off most of the oil leaving just 1–2 tablespoons. Add the paste mixture and cook, stirring frequently, for 1–2 minutes, then stir in the remaining coconut cream, boiling water, lime leaves and second measure of lemongrass. Bring the mixture to the boil and stir in the soy sauce and brown sugar, then remove from the heat.

Arrange the chicken pieces in a large casserole dish. Pour the sauce over the chicken, cover the dish tightly and bake at 180°C for 40 minutes or until chicken is very tender, turning the chicken once after about 20 minutes.

Serve with rice and roti and a simple green salad.

Bacon Wrapped Chicken Breasts

Although there are several steps involved in this recipe, none of them are complicated and the end results are well worth the effort. In fact, this dish makes a good 'dinner party' main, because all the preparation can be done in advance.

For 4 servings:
3 tablespoons olive oil
4 cloves garlic, crushed, peeled and
    chopped
150–200g mushrooms, sliced
125–150g frozen spinach, thawed
about 100g feta, crumbled
½ teaspoon salt
pepper to taste
4 medium (about 1kg total) skinless,
    boneless chicken breasts
8 rashers streaky bacon
4 teaspoons truffle- or porcini-infused
    olive oil

Preheat the oven to 200°C. Heat the oil in a medium non-stick pan. Add the garlic and mushrooms. Cook over a moderate heat, stirring frequently, until the mushrooms have softened, then remove from the heat.

Squeeze most of the liquid from the spinach and stir it into the mushroom mixture. Add the crumbled feta, salt and pepper to taste and stir to combine.

Place the chicken breasts top down on a board, then from the side, cut a pocket into the middle of each. Stuff as much of the spinach mixture into the pocket as you can. (Depending on the size of the breasts and the size of the pockets you may have some filling left.) Wrap each breast up in two rashers of the bacon, using these to hold the pocket shut.

Place the wrapped chicken in a teflon or baking paper-lined roasting pan, drizzle each one with a teaspoon of infused oil and bake for 30–35 minutes or until the bacon is golden brown.

Serve with Garlicky Roast Potatoes (see below) and lightly cooked vegetables or a salad.

Garlicky Roast Potatoes

1kg potatoes, peeled • 2–3 cloves of garlic, crushed and peeled • 2–3 tablespoons olive or canola oil

Cut the potatoes into 2cm cubes. Place in a plastic bag and add the garlic and oil. Toss to combine, then spread the cubes over the bottom of a teflon or baking paper-lined roasting pan.

Cook at 200°C for 25–30 minutes, stirring once or twice, until golden brown.

Crispy Coated Chicken Strips

I guess this is really an oven-baked version of fried chicken, and using the cornflakes makes the coating really crisp and three dimensional.

Since you are already using the oven, why not cook some potato wedges, which make an ideal accompaniment, at the same time. Just add a simple salad, like coleslaw, for a complete meal.

For 4 servings:

800g–1kg skinless, boneless chicken
   breasts or thighs
1/2 cup flour
1 teaspoon garlic salt
1 large egg
1 tablespoon water
1 cup cornflakes, crushed
2 slices bread, crumbed (about 1 cup)
2 teaspoons paprika
1 teaspoon curry powder
1–2 tablespoons olive or other oil

Preheat the oven to 200°C. While the oven heats, cut each chicken breast or thigh lengthwise into two or three strips (depending on original size), then set aside.

Coating the chicken is done in three stages (first flour, then egg, then crumbs), so prepare these mixtures before you proceed any further. Measure the flour and garlic salt into a large plastic bag and shake to combine. Whisk the egg and water together in a flat shallow bowl (a dessert or soup plate works well). Measure the cornflakes into a medium plastic bag and crush them lightly with your hands – you don't want them too big, but you don't want to reduce them to dust either. Add the breadcrumbs, paprika and curry powder and shake the bag until well mixed.

Working one or two strips at a time, drop the chicken into the flour mixture and toss the bag until evenly coated. Shake off excess flour and arrange the chicken pieces on a dry surface, repeat until all chicken is floured. Again working one or two strips at a time, dip floured chicken pieces into the egg mixture, turning to coat evenly, then drop them into the bag of crumb coating, and gently shake the bag until evenly coated.

Arrange the crumbed chicken in a large non-stick, teflon or baking paper-lined roasting dish or sponge roll tin and drizzle lightly with the oil. Bake for 12–15 minutes or until golden brown and the thickest piece is no longer pink in the middle when cut through.

Serve with Potato Wedges (see below) and coleslaw.

Potato Wedges

4–6 medium potatoes • 2–3 tablespoons olive or canola oil • 1/2–1 teaspoon paprika • garlic salt and black pepper to taste

Preheat the oven to 200°C. Quarter potatoes lengthwise (allow 1–1 1/2 medium potatoes per person), then cut each quarter lengthwise into three wedges. Place wedges in a plastic bag and toss with the oil. Arrange wedges in a single layer on a sprayed non-stick or teflon or baking paper-lined tray. Sprinkle lightly with paprika and garlic salt, and pepper to taste, then bake for 15–20 minutes or until golden brown.

Pasta with Chicken, Tomato & Mozzarella Sauce

I like to serve this sauce tossed through fresh fettuccine, but as with most pasta and sauce dishes, you can use any type or shape of pasta that takes your fancy.

You can use dried pasta but put it on to cook first, before you begin to make the sauce, and your timing should be about right.

For 4 servings:
2 tablespoons olive oil
1 medium onion
500g skinless, boneless chicken
    breast or thighs
400g can diced tomatoes in juice
1 tablespoon balsamic vinegar
salt and black pepper to taste
1/4–1/2 cup chopped basil
about 400g fresh pasta
1–2 tablespoons butter
125–150g mozzarella, diced or grated

Heat 1 tablespoon of the olive oil in a large non-stick pan. While the oil heats, quarter, peel and slice the onion. Add the onion to the pan and cook, stirring frequently, until it has softened and begins to brown.

As the onion cooks, cut the chicken into 2cm cubes, add it to the pan and stir-fry until the chicken has lost its pink colour. Stir in the tomatoes and juice, vinegar and salt and pepper to taste.

Simmer the mixture gently until the chicken is just cooked through (cut one of the largest pieces in half to test – it's done when there's no pink in the centre), then stir in about two thirds of the basil.

Put the pasta on to cook in plenty of lightly salted, rapidly boiling water. When al dente, drain and return to the pot and add the remaining oil and the butter. Toss together so the pasta is evenly coated.

Stir the mozzarella into the simmering tomato sauce, then remove from the heat. Either add the sauce to the pasta and toss everything gently together to combine or arrange the cooked pasta on a (warmed) serving platter and pour the sauce over the top. Garnish with the remaining basil and perhaps a grind of pepper, then serve. Crusty bread and a simple green salad make ideal accompaniments.

Chicken & Kumara Curry

To me, this dish falls into the category of a 'winter warmer'. I use mild rather than hot curry powder so it has a good flavour, without any real heat, which my children find quite acceptable.

It makes a large casserole which can be made ahead of time and reheated when required (the flavour only really gets better with standing), so it is useful if expecting company, or alternatively, it will feed a smaller family for two nights.

For 4–6 servings:

6 (about 1.5kg total) chicken thighs
1 tablespoon canola or olive oil
2 large onions
3 cloves garlic, crushed, peeled and chopped
2–3cm piece fresh ginger, peeled and chopped
2 tablespoons mild curry powder
2 whole star anise
5cm cinnamon stick
2 stalks lemongrass, bruised (optional)
500g kumara, peeled
3/4 cup coconut cream
1–1 1/2 cups hot water
2 tablespoons dark soy sauce
salt to taste
2 teaspoons cornflour
2–3 tablespoons chopped coriander

Trim any obvious flaps of excess skin and fat off the thighs, then heat the oil in a large casserole dish. Working in two batches, brown the chicken pieces lightly on both sides, then remove and set aside.

While the chicken browns, peel, quarter and slice the onions. Once the chicken has been removed, add the onions, garlic and ginger to the dish and cook, stirring occasionally, until the onion is soft and beginning to brown. Stir in the curry powder, star anise, cinnamon stick and lemongrass and cook for a minute or so longer.

Cut the kumara into 2–3cm cubes and add to the dish. Stir again, then add the coconut cream, 1 cup of water and the soy sauce. Stir, then return the chicken pieces to the dish, nestling them in so they are mainly covered. Bring the mixture to the boil, then cover with a close-fitting lid. Either reduce the heat to a very gentle simmer or transfer to the oven preheated to 180°C and cook for 30–40 minutes, stirring once or twice (add the extra 1/2 cup of water if you think the mixture is beginning to look dry), until the chicken is very tender.

Once cooked, add salt to taste and if you think the mixture is too thin, mix the cornflour to a paste with a little cold water then stir it into the casserole and simmer a few minutes longer until thickened.

Just before serving stir in most of the chopped coriander, reserving a little to use as a garnish. Serve accompanied by plain rice and naan bread or roti.

Easy Malay-style Chicken Curry

I love Malaysian food and have tried several times to recreate some of the dishes I've enjoyed in restaurants – I think this is my best effort yet! An additional bonus is that it is actually very simple.

I like to make this dish with a mild rather than hot curry powder, which gives it plenty of flavour without being overpowering.

For 3–4 servings:

1 medium onion
2 large cloves garlic
2cm piece ginger
1 tablespoon water
1 tablespoon canola (or other) oil
500g skinless, boneless chicken
　breasts or thighs
3–4 teaspoons mild curry powder
6cm cinnamon stick
1 whole star anise
1 cup regular or lite coconut cream
3/4 cup water
1 teaspoon instant chicken stock
1 tablespoon light soy sauce
1/2 teaspoon each sugar and salt
3–4 tablespoons chopped coriander

Peel and roughly chop the onion, garlic and ginger, then put them into a blender or food processor with the first measure of water. Blend or process to a paste.

Heat the oil in a large non-stick pan. Halve or quarter the chicken breasts or thighs, depending on their size, then add to the pan and cook for about 2 minutes per side or until lightly browned (it does not need to be cooked through at this stage). Remove chicken from the pan and set aside.

Add the onion paste to the pan and cook for 3–4 minutes stirring frequently, then add the curry powder, cinnamon stick and star anise and cook, stirring continuously, for another minute. Stir in the all the remaining ingredients except the coriander, then add the chicken back to the pan. Bring the mixture to the boil then reduce the heat to a gentle simmer and cook for 10–12 minutes or until the chicken is cooked through and the sauce has thickened a little. Stir in most of the coriander reserving a little to use as a garnish.

Serve over rice garnished with the remaining coriander and accompanied by steamed vegetables and roti.

Smoky Chicken Burritos

In Mexico, rather than the few (often anonymous) varieties of chillies we have here, there are many different varieties to choose from. These are known for their different 'heats', flavours and other characteristics. I am by no means an expert in these, but one variety I have tried and like is chipotles, which have an incredible smoky flavour.

Sadly, in this neck of the woods, chipotles are hard to come by, but I have found that by using both smoked paprika (comparatively widely available) and 'regular' chilli powder, I can achieve a similar effect.

For 4 servings:

1 tablespoon canola (or other vegetable) oil
1 large onion
2 cloves garlic
500–600g skinless, boneless chicken breasts or thighs
1 teaspoon smoked paprika
1 teaspoon ground cumin
1/2 teaspoon chilli powder (or more to taste)
1/2 teaspoon oregano
1/4–1/2 cup water
1 teaspoon instant chicken stock
400g can diced tomatoes in juice
1/2 teaspoon salt
1/2 teaspoon sugar
about 1/2 a medium lettuce, finely shredded
1 medium–large carrot, grated
100–150g cheese, grated
chopped coriander
sour cream
12–16 soft flour tortillas (depending on size)

Heat the oil in a large non-stick pan. While the oil heats, quarter and slice the onion and crush, peel and chop the garlic. Add these to the pan and cook, stirring frequently, until soft.

Slice or dice the chicken and add to the pan. Stir-fry for 2–3 minutes or until it has lost its pink colour. Stir in the spices and oregano and cook for about a minute longer.

Add the 1/4 cup of water, instant stock, the tomatoes and their juice, salt and sugar. Stir and allow the mixture to come to the boil, then reduce the heat to a fairly gentle simmer and cook for 5–10 minutes longer, until the thickest pieces of chicken are cooked through and the sauce has thickened, adding more water if the mixture begins to look dry.

While the chicken cooks, prepare the remaining ingredients. I like to arrange them on a platter or in separate bowls and allow people to assemble their own burritos at the table. Just before serving heat the tortillas according to package instructions (or place them in a loosely sealed plastic bag and microwave for about a minute).

To assemble, lie a burrito on a plate, spread a spoonful of the chicken and sauce across the middle, then sprinkle on some lettuce, carrot and cheese. Finish with some coriander and a blob of sour cream, then roll up, wrap in a napkin to prevent spillage and enjoy!

Beer Braised Chicken

This is essentially an 'oven-friendly' version of an American concept. In the original version, the chicken is spice rubbed, then stood, balanced on its end with an opened can of beer in the cavity, and cooked in a large kettle-style barbecue.

While you could in fact do this in an oven, I think it is easier to lie the chicken down and pour the beer around it in a smallish roasting pan. (You could cook it this way on a covered barbecue too.) In terms of flavour you would never really guess that this chicken is cooked sitting in beer, but it does keep the flesh remarkably moist and tender.

For 6 servings:
Marinade
2–3 cloves garlic, peeled
2 tablespoons roughly chopped fresh
   herbs (thyme, basil, rosemary,
   marjoram etc.)
2 teaspoons paprika
2 tablespoons olive oil
1/2 teaspoon salt
pepper to taste
pinch chilli powder (optional)

1.8 kg chicken
330ml can of lager (or your favourite
   light beer)

Blend or crush the marinade ingredients together to make a thin paste. Wash and dry the chicken, inside and out, then rub the cavity and skin with the marinade paste. Place in a 20 x 30cm oven dish and leave to stand while the oven heats (or for longer if time allows, refrigerating if more than 20–30 minutes).

Preheat the oven to 180°C. Pour the beer into the roasting dish around the chicken, then cook uncovered for 50–60 minutes until well browned and the juices run clear when a thigh is pierced at the thickest part.

Serve with a green salad and/or rice salad if the weather is warm, or roast vegetables if the weather is cooler.

Crispy Roasted Thighs on Mushrooms

Infused olive oils are now finding their way out of more exclusive stores and onto regular supermarket shelves. While they are definitely more expensive than 'regular' olive oil they have concentrated flavour and are meant to be used sparingly – so a little really does go a long way.

While you can make this dish quite successfully using unflavoured oil, just a couple of teaspoons of porcini- (or truffle) infused oil really brings out the mushroom flavours and aromas.

For 3–4 servings:
2 tablespoons olive oil
1 large onion
2 cloves garlic
500g mushrooms
2 teaspoons flour
about 1 tablespoon each fresh thyme,
   marjoram and rosemary
4–6 chicken thighs
1/4 cup dry white wine
2–3 teaspoons porcini- (or truffle)
   infused olive oil or plain olive oil
1/2 teaspoon salt
pepper to taste

Preheat the oven to 180°C. Heat the oil in a medium pan. While oil heats, peel, quarter and slice the onion and crush, peel and chop the garlic. Add the onion and garlic to the pan and sauté until the onion has softened but not browned.

While the onion cooks, quarter the mushrooms and spread them over the bottom of a casserole dish or roasting pan just big enough to hold the chicken thighs in a single layer. When the onion mixture is cooked, add it to the mushrooms, sprinkle in the flour, mix to combine then scatter with the herbs.

Trim any excess flaps of fat and skin from the thighs, then arrange these in a single layer over the mushrooms. Pour in the wine and drizzle the infused oil over the thighs. Sprinkle the salt evenly over the surface and add pepper to taste then bake for 30–40 minutes or until the chicken has browned.

Serve with pasta or rice, lightly cooked green vegetables or a salad.

Thanksgiving Thighs

Not surprisingly, I came across the original version of this recipe in an American cookbook. I thought it sounded like an interesting combination of flavours so decided to have a fiddle and this was the result...

The quantities are quite large (it was obviously intended to serve a fairly large group at Thanksgiving dinner) but as it can be prepared in advance and baked at the last minute, this makes it well suited to entertaining friends at any time.

For 6 servings:

2 tablespoons olive or canola oil
1 medium onion, peeled and finely
   diced
2–3 sticks celery, thinly sliced
1 medium apple, cored and finely diced
1 cup walnuts, finely chopped
2 teaspoons chopped fresh sage
   (or 1/2 teaspoon dried)
1 teaspoon chopped fresh thyme
   (or 1/2 teaspoon dried)
1/2 cup dried cranberries, chopped
12 (1.2–1.4kg total) skinless, boneless
   chicken thighs
1/4 cup white wine
1–2 tablespoons olive or canola oil
1/2–1 teaspoon salt
pepper to taste

Heat the first measure of oil in a large pan. Add the onion and celery and cook, stirring frequently, until softened. Stir in the apple, walnuts and herbs then cook for 1–2 minutes longer. Remove the pan from the heat and stir in the cranberries.

Working one at a time, place the chicken thighs between two sheets of plastic and bang gently with the side of a meat hammer or a rolling pin until they are half their original thickness.

Spread 2–3 tablespoons of the filling mixture along one short edge of each flattened thigh and roll up to form a cylinder. Arrange the filled thighs in a shallow, non-stick sprayed casserole or baking dish (about 20 x 30cm). Sprinkle any left-over filling mixture over the chicken, then pour in the wine, drizzle with the second measure of oil and season with salt and pepper.

Refrigerate until required, or transfer immediately to a preheated oven and bake at 180°C for 30–40 minutes until the juices of the largest roll run clear when pierced with a skewer.

Serve with mashed potatoes, lightly cooked vegetables or a simple green salad.

Oriental Braised Chicken

This recipe is a really quick and tasty alternative to 'plain' roasted chicken legs. Not surprisingly the soy and spices give it an Asian feel, so why not carry this through and serve it with rice and Asian-style vegetables.

For 4 servings:

4 whole (thigh and drumstick) chicken
    legs
2 cloves garlic, crushed, peeled and
    chopped
1cm piece ginger, peeled and grated
1/2 cup dark soy sauce
2 tablespoons brown sugar
2 tablespoons sherry
1 tablespoon sesame oil
1 teaspoon cornflour
1 dried chilli
2 whole star anise

Make 3–4 deep (to the bone) slashes across each of the chicken legs, then arrange them in a casserole dish just big enough to hold them in a single layer (non-stick spray this first to make cleaning up easier).

Combine the remaining ingredients and pour over the chicken. Turn the pieces several times so they are well coated, then leave to stand for 10–15 minutes while the oven heats to 180°C.

Arrange the legs skin side down, then cover the casserole and bake for 20 minutes, then uncover. Turn the chicken skin side up, and bake for a further 20 minutes until glossy and brown.

Serve with Coconut Rice (see below) and lightly cooked broccoli (or broccolini) or bok choy.

Coconut Rice

1 1/2 cups jasmine or basmati rice • 2 1/4 cups boiling water • 3/4 cup coconut cream • 1 teaspoon sugar • 1/2 teaspoon salt

Measure all the ingredients into a large microwave bowl. Cover and microwave on medium (50%) for 15–17 minutes or until rice is tender. Leave to stand for 5 minutes, then fluff with a fork before serving.

Chicken with Hokkien Noodles

I recommend fresh Hokkien noodles if you can buy them. As well as being delicious, they just need heating through which makes them very quick to prepare. As with any stir-fry, it pays to have everything cut up ready to go before you start to cook as it all happens so fast once you do start.,

For 4 servings:

500g fresh Hokkien (yellow egg)
    noodles
1 medium onion
1 tablespoon canola (or other) oil
400g skinless, boneless chicken, sliced
    1cm thick (breasts, tenderloins or
    thighs)
1 tablespoon grated ginger
2 tablespoons light soy sauce
2 tablespoons oyster sauce
1 medium carrot, julienned
250g bok choy or spinach, washed
    and separated into individual leaves
1/4 cup sherry
1/2 cup chicken stock (or 1/2 cup water
    plus 1/2 teaspoon instant stock
    powder)
chopped coriander leaf to garnish
    (optional)

Prepare the noodles by teasing them apart, then placing them in a sieve and rinsing with boiling water.

Halve and peel the onion and cut into 5mm slices while you heat the oil in a large pan or wok. Add the onion and cook until softened then add the chicken and ginger. Cook, stirring frequently, until the chicken is lightly browned, then add the soy sauce, oyster sauce and vegetables. Stir-fry for 1–2 minutes, then add the noodles, sherry and stock (or water plus instant stock) and toss everything together.

Cook, tossing occasionally, for a further 3–4 minutes until the vegetables are tender, most of the liquid has gone and the noodles are hot through. Pile into bowls, top with a little chopped coriander and serve immediately.

Spaghetti with Creamy Chicken & Mushroom Sauce

This dish came into being one evening as I surveyed the contents of the refrigerator. Somehow the idea of a pale creamy mushroom sauce appealed and the rest, as they say, is history.

For 2–3 servings:
3 tablespoons olive oil
1 medium onion
250g mushrooms
1 tablespoon chopped fresh thyme
black pepper to taste
250–300g chicken mince
250–300g spaghetti
1/4 cup sherry
1/4 cup water
1/2 cup cream
1/2 teaspoon salt
1–2 teaspoons olive oil
1 tablespoon butter

Heat 2 tablespoons of olive oil in a large, preferably non-stick, pan. While the oil heats, peel and dice the onion, then add it to the pan and cook, stirring occasionally, until the onion has softened. Cut the mushrooms into 5–7mm slices (you can use white or brown mushrooms, or a mixture, but remember the darker the mushrooms, the darker the sauce), then add them to the softened onions and continue to cook, stirring occasionally, until the mushrooms have wilted. Add the thyme and a generous grind of black pepper and cook for a minute longer.

Remove the onion and mushroom mixture from the pan and heat the remaining tablespoon of oil. Add the chicken mince and cook over a high heat, stirring frequently to break up any lumps, for about 3–4 minutes or until the chicken is lightly browned.

While the chicken cooks, bring a large pot of lightly salted water to the boil and put the spaghetti on to cook.

Add the onion and mushroom mixture to the chicken, then stir in the sherry, water, cream and salt. Allow the sauce to come to the boil then reduce the heat and leave to simmer gently while the pasta cooks.

Drain the cooked pasta, transfer it back to the cooking pot and toss it together with a dash of olive oil and the butter. Add the sauce to the pasta and toss gently to evenly combine. Divide between serving plates and serve garnished with a sprig or two of thyme and a grind of pepper and accompanied with a simple green salad and maybe some crusty bread.

Alternatively, arrange the pasta on a warmed serving platter then top with the sauce mixture.

Chicken with Lemon & Rosemary

Lemon and rosemary combine to make this fragrant chicken dish decidedly different. The cooking process is a two-step one – pan browning, then baking – but it's pretty simple really and once they're in the oven you can put your feet up for a while.

For 3–4 servings:
2 lemons
3–4 x 5cm sprigs rosemary
3–4 x 5cm sprigs thyme
2 cloves garlic, peeled
6 chicken thighs
1 tablespoons olive oil
2–3 tablespoons flour
salt and pepper to taste

Preheat the oven to 200°C. Thinly peel the yellow zest from the lemons with a potato peeler (or grate finely). Place it in a blender or mortar and pestle, add the next three ingredients and blend or grind together until well mixed.

Trim any flaps of excess skin and fat from the thighs. Using a finger, poke a tunnel down between the skin and flesh of each thigh and push a little of the herb and lemon mixture into each (use it all up).

Heat the oil in a large non-stick pan. Place the thighs skin-side down in the pan and cook, shaking the pan occasionally to make sure the chicken doesn't stick, until golden brown. (Depending on the size of the pan, you may need to do this in two batches.)

Arrange the thighs, skin-side up, in a non-stick sprayed ovenproof dish just large enough to hold them. Sprinkle them with the flour and salt and pepper to taste. Squeeze the juice of the lemons over the chicken and bake for 20–30 minutes until well browned and the juices run clear when pierced.

Serve with pasta or potato wedges (cooked at the same time, see page 68) and a salad.

Tuscan Baked Chicken with Tomatoes & Olives

This dish gives a taste of summer at any time of the year. Serve with pasta and a simple salad in warm weather, or replace the salad with cooked vegetables if it's cooler.

For 4 servings:
1 tablespoon olive oil
4 boneless (skin on) chicken breasts
1 medium onion, quartered, peeled
    and sliced
1 large clove garlic, crushed, peeled
    and chopped
1 medium red capsicum (pepper),
    deseeded and diced
2 x 400g cans diced tomatoes in juice
2 tablespoons balsamic vinegar
1/2 teaspoon salt
pepper to taste
about 1/4 cup chopped basil or
    1–2 tablespoons basil pesto
1/2 cup kalamata olives
parmesan cheese (optional)

Preheat the oven to 180°C. Heat the oil in a large non-stick pan. Add the chicken breasts and cook for 3–4 minutes per side, or until lightly browned. Remove the chicken from the pan and arrange the pieces skin-side up in a large (non-stick sprayed) casserole dish.

Stir the onion and garlic into the pan and cook, stirring occasionally, until the onion has softened. Add the capsicum and cook, stirring frequently, for 2–3 minutes longer. Add the next six ingredients and bring to the boil, stirring occasionally.

Pour the sauce over the chicken, sprinkle with grated parmesan if desired, then transfer to the oven and bake uncovered for 25–30 minutes.

Serve over pasta, accompanied with a salad or vegetables and some crusty bread.

Sweet & Spicy Chicken Drumsticks

Although neither ingredient tastes particularly sweet by itself, the addition of a little coconut cream to a tomato-based sauce like the one in this recipe, always seems to add a hint of sweetness.

For 4 servings:
2 tablespoons canola (or other) oil
8 (about 1.2kg) chicken drumsticks
1 medium onion, peeled and diced
2 cloves garlic, crushed, peeled and
    chopped
2–3 tablespoons grated ginger
5cm cinnamon stick
6–8 cloves
4 whole cardamom pods, flattened
2 bay leaves
2 teaspoons curry powder (mild or hot
    to taste)
400g can diced tomatoes in juice
165g can (½ cup) coconut cream
about 2 tablespoons chopped
    coriander
sautéed slivered almonds and currants
    to garnish (optional)

Heat 1 tablespoon of the oil in a large casserole dish. Add the chicken drumsticks and fry, turning occasionally, until golden brown on all sides (about 6–8 minutes).

Remove and set aside the chicken and add the remaining oil, onion and garlic to the casserole dish. Cook, stirring occasionally, for about 5 minutes until the onion is soft and beginning to brown. Add the ginger, whole spices and bay leaves, stir and cook for a minute longer. Add the curry powder and cook, stirring continuously, for another minute before adding the chicken, tomatoes and coconut cream.

Allow the mixture to come to the boil, then reduce the heat, cover and simmer gently for 20–30 minutes, stirring occasionally, until the meat begins to fall from the bones.

While the chicken cooks, prepare some steamed rice and poppadums. When the chicken is cooked, add salt to taste and stir in the chopped coriander.

Serve over steamed rice garnished with a few sautéed slivered almonds and currants (if desired) and accompany with poppadums.

Stir-fried Chicken & Broccoli with Chilli Almonds

I have come to the conclusion that with stir-fries the key to success is often simplicity. Rather than trying to cram in relatively small quantities of all sorts of different vegetables, I now prefer to add a larger quantity of one or maybe two varieties instead – as I have here. I think the results speak for themselves.

For 2–3 servings:
2 teaspoons chilli oil (or 'plain' oil)
½ cup whole unblanched almonds
250–300g skinless, boneless chicken
    breast, cubed
1 clove garlic, peeled and chopped
1cm ginger, peeled and julienned
2 teaspoons canola oil
1 medium–large head broccoli, cut into
    florets
1 tablespoon water
2 tablespoons Kikkoman soy sauce
1 tablespoon sherry
1 teaspoon cornflour
1 teaspoon hot chilli sauce
1 teaspoon brown sugar
1–2 tablespoons water, if required

Heat the first measure of oil in a large frypan or wok. Add almonds and cook, stirring frequently, until the almonds have browned visibly (about 3–5 minutes). Remove from pan with slotted spoon.

Add chicken to the pan along with the garlic and ginger and stir-fry for about 3 minutes or until lightly browned on all sides, then tip into a plate or bowl and set aside.

Return pan to the heat and add the second measure of oil. When oil is hot add the broccoli florets and water and stir-fry until bright green and just tender.

Combine the soy sauce, sherry, cornflour, chilli sauce and sugar, then add to the pan along with the chicken. Toss to combine and cook, stirring frequently, for 1–2 minutes longer, adding a tablespoon or two of water if you think it looks too dry.

Serve over rice or noodles.

lamb &
beef

Filo Lamb Packages

These crispy, golden little filo packages are absolutely irresistible. By keeping the parcels small, you can avoid having to precook the lamb filling, which means they're also quick to make.

Sumac is a red wine-coloured, slightly crystalline-looking Middle Eastern seasoning. It has a fruity, tangy flavour that makes a nice addition to this recipe if you have it, but it can be omitted without any dire effects.

For 4 servings:

1 tablespoon olive oil
1 medium onion, peeled and diced
2 cloves garlic, peeled and chopped
1/4 cup pinenuts
1/2 cup currants
400g minced lamb
2 teaspoons ground cumin
2 teaspoons sumac (optional)
1/2 teaspoon cinnamon
1 large egg
1/4 cup chopped parsley
1/2 teaspoon salt
black pepper to taste
8–10 sheets filo pastry
2 tablespoons olive oil or melted butter

Preheat the oven to 170°C. Heat the oil in a medium frypan. Add the onion and garlic and cook, stirring frequently, for about 5 minutes until the onion is soft. Stir in the pinenuts and currants and cook for 2–3 minutes longer, or until the pinenuts are lightly browned and the currants have puffed up.

Put the mince, spices, egg and parsley in a large bowl, add the cooked onion mixture and stir until everything is well combined. Add the salt and pepper to taste, then mix again to combine.

Lay a sheet of filo pastry on a clean, dry surface. Lightly brush the length of one side with oil or melted butter then fold the sheet in half lengthwise to make a long rectangle. Place a 1/4 cup of the lamb mixture near one end (avoid being over generous or the packages will be hard to shape and may burst during cooking) and then diagonally fold one corner over the filling to make a pointy end. Fold the pointy end and the filling up to make the end square again. Continue folding until you are left with a triangular package. Brush the outside with a little more oil or butter, then place the package on a non-stick sprayed or teflon-lined baking tray. Repeat this process until all the filling is used and you have 8–10 packages.

Place the packages in the oven and bake for 15 minutes, reducing the heat a little if they look like they're browning too much (don't take the packages out too soon because the filling has to cook through).

Serve with rice or plain or Fruity Couscous (see page 56) and a green or tomato salad.

Szechwan Pepper & Spice Marinated Lamb Racks

Something a little different to try with lamb racks – Szechwan pepper, star anise and ginger give a mild but decidedly Asian flavour to a traditional favourite. I like to serve these with rice and vegetables that also have an oriental flavour to enhance the effect.

For 2–4 servings:
Marinade
1 teaspoon Szechwan peppercorns
2 whole star anise
2¹/2cm cinnamon stick
1 medium dried chilli
¹/2 teaspoon five spice powder
2 cloves garlic, peeled and chopped
2¹/2cm piece fresh ginger, peeled and
   finely sliced
¹/2 cup hot water
¹/4 cup brown sugar
2 tablespoons dark soy sauce
1 tablespoon sesame oil

2–4 chined lamb racks
1 teaspoon cornflour
1 tablespoon cold water

Toast peppercorns in a small pot until they are fragrant and begin to smoke. Transfer to a mortar and pestle and grind, then return to the pot. Add the remaining marinade ingredients and heat, stirring occasionally, until boiling, then reduce the heat and simmer for 3–5 minutes. Remove from the heat and leave to stand for a few minutes while you prepare the lamb.

Cut most (but not all) of the outer fat layer off the lamb racks, then lightly score in a diagonal pattern. Lie racks scored side down on a flat shallow dish just big enough to hold them, then pour over the marinade. Leave to stand for 20–30 minutes or refrigerate overnight, turning once or twice.

Preheat the oven to 200°C. Transfer the lamb racks to a non-stick roasting pan and cover the exposed ends of the rib bones with foil. Place the pan in the middle of the oven and cook for 14–16 minutes (depending on the thickness and how well you like it done), then remove from oven and leave to stand for about 5 minutes before serving. While the lamb cooks, mix the cornflour and water to a paste and stir it into the remaining (strained) marinade, and heat until it boils and thickens to use as a sauce for the cooked lamb.

Serve with Coconut Rice (see page 78) and Sesame Cabbage (see below).

Sesame Cabbage

2–4 tablespoons water • ¹/4–¹/2 small cabbage, thinly sliced • 1–2 tablespoons butter • 1–2 teaspoons sesame oil • black pepper to taste

Heat the water in a large lidded pan or pot and bring to the boil. Add the cabbage and cook, stirring occasionally, until just cooked. Add the butter, sesame oil and black pepper to taste, toss to combine and serve.

Jerk Lamb with Kiwifruit Salsa

Caribbean and Jamaican flavours are among the 'hot' (fashion-wise that is) flavours presently. The seasonings in this Jamaican Jerk mixture go well with the semi-tropical flavours of the kiwifruit in the salsa.

If you want to try something a little different, add some wedges of grilled fresh pineapple – it goes well with both the lamb and salsa and adds to the Caribbean feel.

For 3–4 servings:
Marinade
½ small onion
2 cloves garlic, peeled
2 tablespoons olive or canola oil
1 tablespoon lime or lemon juice
1 tablespoon brown sugar
1 teaspoon paprika
1 teaspoon ground cumin
1 teaspoon thyme
½–1 teaspoon chilli powder, to taste
½ teaspoon allspice
½ teaspoon cinnamon
½ teaspoon salt

About 750g lamb fillets

Salsa
4 green kiwifruit, diced
2 cloves garlic, peeled and chopped
2 tablespoons Thai sweet chilli sauce
2 tablespoons lemon or lime juice
½ teaspoon salt
2–3 tablespoons chopped coriander

Put the onion, garlic, oil and lime or lemon juice in a blender or food processor and process until smooth. Add the remaining marinade ingredients and mix again.

Place the lamb in a plastic bag, then add the marinade mixture. Massage the bag so the meat is covered, then seal the bag, squeezing out as much air as possible. Leave to stand for at least an hour.

Preheat the grill (or barbecue). While it heats, prepare the salsa. Peel the kiwifruit and cut the flesh into 5–7mm cubes, place in a small bowl, add the remaining salsa ingredients and stir gently to combine. Leave to stand while the lamb cooks.

Gently shake any excess marinade off the lamb. Place it on a wire rack and grill close (5–10cm) to the heat for 3–4 minutes per side (or barbecue on a lightly oiled hot plate) until browned and cooked to your liking – slice through the thickest part of one fillet to check. Leave to stand for 3–4 minutes before slicing diagonally.

Serve the lamb drizzled with salsa and accompanied with plain or Coconut Rice (see page 78).

Variation: *Try replacing lamb fillets with shoulder chops and adding a mashed kiwifruit to the marinade mixture to help tenderise the meat.*

Pide (Turkish Pizza)

Turkey was a fascinating and memorable country to visit for many different reasons, not the least of which was the food. Although we were on tight 'backpacker' budgets we were still able to eat well.

One hotel we stayed in had a small outdoor kitchen, complete with a wood-fired oven from which they would produce delicious pide, or Turkish pizza. These have stuck in the back of my mind ever since, but I've only begun to play round with the idea relatively recently.

For 4 pide (4–6 servings):
1 pizza dough recipe (see below)
1 tablespoon olive or canola oil
1 medium onion, peeled and diced
500g minced lamb
1/4 cup currants
1 teaspoon paprika
1/2 teaspoon mint
1/2 teaspoon cinnamon
1/4 teaspoon chilli powder, optional
1/2 teaspoon salt
2 cups (200g) grated cheddar or
   crumbled feta cheese
4 eggs

Preheat the oven to 200°C. Working on a lightly floured surface, divide the pizza dough into four equal portions. Roll each portion into a ball, then roll each ball into an oval about 30cm long and 20cm wide. Place the ovals on non-stick sprayed or lightly oiled baking sheets (you should be able to get two per sheet), brush the outer edge of each oval with water and fold in 1–2cm of the dough to form a canoe or eye shape. Leave the dough to rise at room temperature while you prepare the filling.

Heat the oil in a large pan. Add the onion and cook for 3–4 minutes, stirring occasionally, until the onion is soft, then add the mince. Cook, stirring frequently to break up any lumps, for about 5 minutes longer, until the lamb is lightly browned. Stir in the next six ingredients and cook for a couple of minutes longer before removing from the heat.

Spread a quarter of the lamb mixture over each of the bases, then sprinkle them evenly with the grated (or crumbled) cheese. Break one of the eggs into a small bowl, whisk it with a fork, then pour the egg evenly over the filling of one pide. Repeat this process until all four are egg-covered.

Place two racks near the middle of the oven, slide in the trays of pide and bake for 12–15 minutes (swap the trays over after about 6 minutes), until the bottoms are lightly browned.

Serve with a simple green or tomato salad.

Pizza Dough

3 teaspoons instant active dried yeast • 1/2 cup milk • 3/4 cup boiling water • 2 teaspoons sugar • 1 1/2 teaspoons salt • 2 tablespoons olive or canola oil • 3 cups high grade flour • additional flour or water if required

If making by hand:

Measure the yeast into a large bowl. Combine the milk and water, and add this to the yeast along with the sugar, salt and oil. Leave to stand for a couple of minutes, then add half the flour and stir well to make a thick batter, then add the remaining flour and stir to make a dough firm enough to knead (add extra flour if required). Tip onto a floured surface and knead for 5–10 minutes, then cover the dough loosely and leave to rise for about 10 minutes before using.

If using a bread machine:

Measure all the ingredients into the machine, set the machine to the 'Dough' cycle and press start. Check the dough after a few minutes of mixing and if it looks too wet add a little extra flour, or a little water if too dry. The dough can be removed from the machine any time after about 30 minutes from the start of mixing or, if you have time, let the cycle run through.

Little Lamb Wellingtons

As the name suggests, these are modelled after their more famous cousin, the Beef Wellington, which is made using a much larger piece of beef fillet and then carved into individual servings. Instead these are made in individual servings using versatile and delicious (if a little pricey) lamb fillets, or loins. I think this puts them to good use and makes a great dish for special occasions.

If you like, you can assemble the packages in advance, refrigerate until required, and then cook them more or less at the last minute – they don't really benefit from standing around once they are done.

For 4 servings:

8–12 spinach leaves
1 teaspoon dried mint or
    2–3 teaspoons chopped fresh mint
4 teaspoons Dijon mustard
2 sheets (about 300g total) pre-rolled
    flakey pastry, thawed
4 largish (about 500g in total) lamb
    fillets
salt and pepper
1 lightly beaten egg to glaze

Begin by preparing all the ingredients. Wash and dry the spinach leaves, then set them aside. Mix the mint through the mustard, then, working on a clean, lightly floured bench, gently roll the pastry sheets out to about one and a half times their original size and cut the sheets in half.

Lamb fillets taper at the ends, so to help ensure they cook evenly, cut them in half (widthwise) at the middle, then lie the two halves side by side with cut ends pointing out – hopefully this will leave you with a cylinder of lamb of roughly uniform thickness. Alternatively, just fold the thinner ends back on the fillet to achieve roughly the same effect.

Brush each lamb fillet all over with about a teaspoon of the mustard mixture, then sprinkle with a pinch of salt and a good grind of black pepper. Place one or two spinach leaves widthwise on the pastry sheet, place a lamb fillet on the spinach and cover with another one or two spinach leaves. Carefully roll each sheet to form a cylindrical parcel, brushing the overlapping end of the pastry with a little water to seal. Gently flatten the pastry at the ends with your hands, pushing out as much air as possible. Trim off any large excess of pastry if required, then fold the last centimetre or so under and 'crimp' the ends with your fingers or using the tines of a fork. Decorate with pastry off-cuts if desired. Refrigerate until required.

When ready to cook, preheat the oven to 200°C. Brush the parcels with egg glaze and bake for 12–15 minutes until golden brown. Leave to stand for 2–3 minutes before serving.

New York-style Meatballs

These are probably the result of watching too much TV – I've always had a strange fascination with the meatball sandwiches (made with enormous, sliced meatballs) that seem to feature on programmes set in New York.

I concocted these purely from the looks of what I have seen, but without any actual experience of the real thing, so cannot really vouch for their authenticity; but I can assure you they're delicious.

**For 4–6 servings
(8–12 large meatballs):**
Meatballs
400g pork mince
400g beef (or veal) mince
2 cloves garlic, crushed, peeled and
    chopped
1 cup fresh breadcrumbs (about
    3 slices bread)
1/2 teaspoon marjoram
1/2 teaspoon oregano
1/2 teaspoon salt
black pepper to taste

Sauce
1 tablespoon olive or other oil
1 medium onion, peeled and diced
2 x 400g cans diced tomatoes in juice
1/2 cup red wine
2 tablespoons tomato paste
1 teaspoon basil
1/2 teaspoon salt
black pepper to taste

1/2–1 cup grated cheese to top
    (optional)

Preheat the oven to 200°C. Put all the meatball ingredients in a large bowl, then, using clean hands, mix until well combined.

Tip the mixture onto a board and divide it into quarters, then divide each quarter into two or three equally-sized pieces (depending on how big you want the finished meatballs). Wet your hands to prevent sticking, then shape each portion into a round ball. Lightly oil or non-stick spray a 20 x 30cm (2.5–3 litre) casserole dish, arrange the meatballs in it and place in the oven for 15 minutes to brown lightly.

While the meatballs brown, prepare the sauce. Heat the oil in a large pan, add the onion and cook, stirring frequently, for about 5 minutes until the onion has softened. Stir in the next five ingredients and add the pepper to taste. Bring the mixture to the boil then reduce the heat and leave to simmer gently.

When the meatballs have browned, remove them from the oven and pour the sauce over and around them. Top with some grated cheese if you like, and return the dish to the oven for another 15–20 minutes.

Serve over pasta accompanied with lightly cooked vegetables or a green salad. Of course, leftovers do make good hot or cold sandwiches.

Thai-style Curried Meatballs

These meatballs are simmered in a creamy Thai-style curry sauce and the results are deliciously different from their more familiar Italian-style cousins. Serve over rice for a quick and delicious meal.

For 4 servings:
500g lean minced beef
2 cloves garlic, crushed, peeled and
    finely chopped
1 tablespoon sweet chilli sauce
1 teaspoon red curry paste
1/2 teaspoon salt
2 tablespoons canola or olive oil
1 medium onion, diced
2 tablespoons red curry paste
3/4 cup coconut cream
1/2 cup hot water
3–4 fresh or dried kaffir lime leaves
1 tablespoon fish sauce
1 medium carrot, julienned
1 cup small broccoli florets or frozen
    peas or beans

Place the mince in a large bowl. Add the garlic, chilli sauce, curry paste and salt and mix or stir until well combined (clean hands do this best). Divide the mixture into quarters, then divide each quarter into six to eight portions and, working with wet hands to prevent sticking, shape the mixture into equally sized balls.

Heat the oil in a large, non-stick pan. Add the meatballs and cook, shaking the pan frequently to prevent sticking and to keep the balls round, until golden brown on all sides. Remove the meatballs from the pan with a fish slice and set aside.

Add the onion to the pan and cook, stirring frequently, until it is soft. Stir in the second measure of curry paste and cook, stirring continuously, for one or two minutes longer, then add the coconut cream, water and lime leaves. Stir thoroughly and bring to the boil, then add the meatballs and fish sauce. Allow the mixture to boil again, then reduce the heat and simmer gently for 5 minutes.

Add the carrot and green vegetables of your choice to the pan, stir gently and simmer for a few minutes longer until the vegetables are just cooked. Serve over steamed rice, with a simple green salad on the side if desired.

Roasted Moroccan Lamb with Lemon & Onion

I think the flavour of lamb works really well with this Moroccan-style seasoning. I add roasted lemons to echo the flavour of the preserved lemons sometimes used in Morocco and the onions, well, just for their colour and flavour.

For 4 servings:
2 cloves garlic, peeled
1 tablespoon olive oil
2 teaspoons ground cumin
1 teaspoon ground coriander
1 teaspoon ground ginger
1/2 teaspoon turmeric
1/2 teaspoon cinnamon
1/2 teaspoon paprika (plain or smoked)
1/4 teaspoon chilli powder
1/2 teaspoon salt

2 lemons
2 medium red onions
2 tablespoons balsamic vinegar
2 tablespoon olive oil
1 teaspoon honey

500–600g lamb back straps or fillets
1–2 teaspoons olive or canola oil

16–20 kalamata (or other) olives

Combine the garlic, olive oil, spices and salt in a food processor, blender or mortar and pestle, and blend to a smooth paste. Scrape the paste into a plastic bag, then add the lamb. Massage the bag so the meat is evenly covered with the spice marinade. Squeeze as much excess air as you can from the bag and then leave to marinate for 20 minutes or longer (refrigerating overnight is fine).

Preheat the oven to heat to 200°C. Wash the lemons in hot water, then cut them each into six wedges. Peel the papery skins from the onions and cut these into thin (1.5–2cm) wedges.

Non-stick spray a large roasting dish (about 20 x 30cm), then add the lemon and onion wedges. Drizzle with the balsamic vinegar, the second measure of oil and honey, then toss them gently so they are evenly coated.

Place the lemon and onion mixture in the heated oven and cook for 15–20 minutes. While they are cooking heat the third measure of oil in a large pan over a high heat. Add the lamb (working in two batches if required), and cook for 2–3 minutes until golden brown on one side, then remove from the pan.

Arrange the lamb, browned side up, over the lemon and onion mixture, scatter the olives over the top, then return to the oven and cook for 8–10 minutes longer, or until the lamb is cooked to your liking.

Remove from the oven and stand for 3–4 minutes before serving with plain or Fruity Couscous (see page 56) and a simple green or tomato salad.

Barbecued Flank Steak Sandwiches

I read somewhere recently that about 70% of all meals prepared at home in the United States are actually sandwiches. While on one level this is pretty alarming, it has to be said that if you take a 'sandwich' seriously (as many Americans do) it can indeed become a meal in its own right.

For 4 servings:
1 medium red onion
2 cloves garlic
1/4 cup lemon juice
2 tablespoons soy sauce
2 teaspoons sesame oil
about 600g flank (skirt) steak
1 medium onion, peeled and sliced
1 tablespoon olive or canola oil
2–3 tablespoons mayonnaise
2–3 tablespoons Dijon mustard
1 French stick
lettuce or mesclun
2–3 ripe tomatoes

Peel and quarter the red onion. Place in a food processor or blender along with the garlic, lemon juice, soy sauce and sesame oil and process or blend until smoothish. Lie the steak on a board. Using a sharp knife, lightly score the surface in a diamond pattern. Turn it over and do the same on the other side. Place the steak in a large, unpunctured plastic bag and pour in the red onion marinade. Massage the bag so both sides of the steak are well covered with the paste, then squeeze out as much air as possible from the bag and leave to marinate for at least 15 minutes.

To cook, preheat a grill plate on a barbecue or a large, heavy frypan on a stove on a high heat. Remove the steak from the bag and gently shake off the excess marinade. Lightly non-stick spray the grill plate (or pan) and add the steak. Cook for 3–4 minutes per side (flank steak needs to be fairly rare or it will be tough), then remove from the heat and set aside for about 5 minutes.

While the steak rests, cook the onion in the oil until soft and beginning to brown, and mix the mayonnaise and mustard together.

To serve, thinly slice the steak across the grain (usually widthwise). If you cut slices holding the knife at about 45 degrees to the board, rather than straight up and down, the cut slices will be much wider and more generous looking.

Split the French stick and spread both sides with the mustard-mayonnaise mixture. Add some lettuce or mesclun, some sliced tomatoes, a layer of the fried onion and a generous layer of the beef. Replace the top of the loaf and serve.

Note: *If a tasty roll or sandwich is not your thing, try this steak marinated and cooked the same way, but served tossed through a generous mound of mixed mesclun and/or other salad greens, and drizzled with an Asian-style dressing (see page 104).*

Lamb in Yoghurt & Honey

This is a simple but slightly different from 'the norm' treatment of good old lamb chops. Serve them as you would normally serve grilled chops, or add the Spicy Potatoes and Raita (see below) for an Indian-style meal.

For 4 servings:
Marinade
1 large clove garlic, peeled
2cm piece ginger, peeled
1/2 cup plain, unsweetened yoghurt
2 tablespoons lemon juice
1 tablespoon honey
2 good-sized sprigs mint
   (or 1 teaspoon dried)
1 teaspoon curry powder
1/2 teaspoon salt

500–600g lamb shoulder or loin chops

Place the marinade ingredients in a blender or food processor and process until smooth and evenly combined.

Arrange the chops in a shallow container in a single layer, then pour in the marinade. Turn the chops so they are coated with the marinade, then leave to stand at room temperature for 10–15 minutes.

To cook, remove the chops from the marinade and arrange them on a rack. Grill about 10cm below the heat for 5–7 minutes per side. Serve with rice and vegetables or Spicy Potatoes (see below).

Spicy Potatoes

600–800g potatoes • 1 teaspoon turmeric • 1 teaspoon salt • 2 tablespoons canola oil • 1 teaspoon mustard seeds • 1 teaspoon cumin seeds • 1 teaspoon each paprika, ground coriander and garam masala • handful curry leaves (optional) • 1/2–1 teaspoon minced red chilli (optional) • 2 tablespoons lemon juice • salt to taste

Scrub the potatoes and cut into 2cm cubes. Place them in a large pot, just cover with hot water, then add the turmeric and salt. Bring to the boil and cook for 8–10 minutes until tender, then drain.

Heat the oil in a large non-stick pan. Add the mustard and cumin seeds and cook until the seeds begin to pop, then stir in the potatoes, ground spices, curry leaves, chilli and lemon juice. Cook for 4–5 minutes stirring frequently, remove from the heat, season to taste and serve.

Raita

1 small carrot, finely cubed • 5–10cm cucumber, deseeded and finely diced • 1/2 cup yoghurt • 1–2 tablespoons finely chopped mint • salt and pepper to taste

Mix all the ingredients in a small bowl. Serve alongside almost any Indian or curry dish.

Rolled Shoulder of Lamb with Tapenade & Almonds

It's true that you can't actually get this onto the table in less than an hour from start to finish, but I think the minimal actual 'hands on' time and the moreish end result justify its inclusion.

I think this works well with almonds, but lightly toasted pinenuts would work well too, and still be in keeping with the Mediterranean flavours.

For 4–6 servings:

½ cup slivered almonds or pine nuts

1–1.25kg boned lamb shoulder or leg

4 tablespoons tapenade, bought or homemade (see below)

2 tablespoons olive oil

2 small onions, peeled and quartered

4–6 cloves garlic, peeled and crushed

1 medium carrot, peeled and roughly chopped

1 cup white wine

1 cup chicken or vegetable stock

2 tablespoons flour

about 1 cup chicken or vegetable stock or water

Preheat the oven to 180°C. Put the almonds or pine nuts in a dry pan and toast over a medium heat, shaking occasionally, until golden brown. Remove from the pan and set aside.

Lie the lamb skin-side down on a board and spread the upward-facing side with the tapenade, then sprinkle evenly with the toasted almonds or pine nuts. Starting at one of the short ends, roll the lamb tightly up into a cylinder and tie with cotton string.

Heat the oil in a large casserole dish or roasting pan and brown the lamb on all sides, then remove from the heat. Arrange the onions, garlic and carrots around the lamb and pour in the wine and stock. Place in the oven and cook uncovered for 1 hour.

Remove from the oven and set the lamb aside to rest. Strain off the liquid and reserve, discarding the vegetables. Place the casserole or roasting dish over a high heat, add the flour plus a tablespoon or so of oil or fat from the reserved liquid and cook, stirring continuously, until the flour is lightly browned. Carefully pour in the remaining reserved liquid and stir until smooth and the gravy boils and thickens. Reduce the heat and thin gravy to the desired consistency with the extra stock or water.

Serve the lamb thickly sliced with roast vegetables and gravy.

Tapenade

For about ½ cup: 1 clove garlic, peeled • 125–150g pitted black olives • 3–4 tablespoons lightly packed fresh parsley • 3–4 anchovy fillets, plus a little of their oil • 1 tablespoon capers • 1 tablespoon olive oil • 1 tablespoon lemon juice • freshly ground black pepper

Place the garlic, olives and parsley in a food processor and process until well chopped. Add the anchovy fillets plus 2–3 teaspoons of the oil they were packed in and the capers. Process again until well mixed. Pour in the olive oil and lemon juice and process to make a smoothish paste (how smooth is up to you). Season with a little freshly ground black pepper.

Place in a clean airtight container and store in the fridge for 1–2 weeks. Use with the shoulder of lamb or serve with crackers or crostini and a selection of chopped fresh vegetables for dipping.

pork

Tex Mex Ribs

I'm not sure whether it's because we spent time in the States when I was a child, or whether it's just some sort of primitive urge, but I love gnawing away on a pile of ribs.

The delicious sauce on these contains some chocolate – an idea I've seen in many Mexican cookery books and thought sounded fascinating, but had never got around to trying before. Chocolate and pork may sound an unusual combination but I think it works well!

For 3–4 servings:
2 tablespoons canola or olive oil
1 medium onion, peeled and finely chopped
2 cloves garlic, crushed, peeled and chopped
1/2 teaspoon chilli powder
1/2 teaspoon ground allspice
1 cup water
6 tablespoons tomato paste
1/4 cup balsamic vinegar
25g (5 squares) dark cooking chocolate
1–1.5kg meaty pork ribs

Preheat the oven to 180°C. Heat the oil in a medium pan. Add the onion and garlic and cook, stirring frequently, until the onion is soft. Stir in the chilli powder and allspice and cook for about a minute, then stir in the water, tomato paste and balsamic vinegar. Allow the mixture to boil, then remove from the heat. Break up the squares of chocolate and add to the mixture, stirring occasionally until the chocolate has melted and is evenly mixed in.

Cut the ribs between the bones so they are in 2–3 rib sections (this makes them more manageable to eat). Thoroughly non-stick spray or baking paper-line a large roasting pan. Spread the ribs over the bottom in a single layer, then pour in the sauce. Turn the ribs several times so they are coated with the sauce.

Place the pan in the middle of the oven and cook for 50–60 minutes, turning the ribs and basting with the sauce after 30 minutes.

Serve with rice or Potato Wedges (see page 68) or mashed potatoes, and a green salad or coleslaw.

Penne with Bacon & Broccoli

Pasta makes a great base for many quick and easy meals. This recipe is no exception – the delicious sauce can easily be prepared while the pasta cooks, meaning you can actually be in and out of the kitchen in 15 minutes or less.

For 2–3 servings:
250–300g penne or other 'short' pasta
2 tablespoons olive oil
1 medium onion, peeled and diced
4 rashers of bacon
1 large head broccoli
1/2 cup cream
1/2–1 teaspoon salt
pepper to taste
1/4 cup pasta cooking water, if required
1/2 cup parmesan

Put the pasta on to cook in plenty of lightly salted boiling water. While the pasta cooks, heat 1 tablespoon of the oil in a medium frypan. Add the onion and cook for 2–3 minutes, stirring frequently, until the onion has softened. While the onion cooks, cut the bacon widthwise into pieces 1cm wide. Stir the bacon into the pan and continue to cook until the bacon is lightly browned.

Cut the broccoli into small florets, add these to the pan and stir-fry for 1–2 minutes longer. Pour in the cream and add salt and pepper to taste. Simmer the sauce, stirring occasionally, until the broccoli is tender through, adding a little pasta cooking water if the mixture begins to look dry, then remove from the heat.

Drain the cooked pasta then return it to its cooking pot. Add the remaining tablespoon of oil and toss or stir gently to mix through. Add the sauce and the grated parmesan to the pasta and toss everything together until evenly mixed. Serve immediately, garnished with a little additional shaved or grated parmesan.

A green or tomato salad and bread make excellent accompaniments.

Pork & Pineapple Curry

I have always had strong reservations about the combination of pork and pineapple, but this combination of savoury, sweet and salty flavours makes my mouth water at the mere thought...

The first few times I made this I used fresh pineapple, but one day I found the fresh pineapple I was planning to use had been eaten, so I used a can of pineapple rings instead. To my surprise they actually worked very well, so if fresh pineapple is out of season, give them a try instead.

For 3–4 servings:
500g lean tender pork (schnitzel, loin etc.) sliced or cubed
2 teaspoons cornflour
2 tablespoons light soy sauce
2 tablespoons medium–dry sherry
1 tablespoon sesame oil
2 tablespoons canola or other oil
1 medium onion, peeled, quartered and sliced
2 tablespoons Thai red curry paste
1/2 small pineapple, peeled and cut in 2cm chunks (or 440g can pineapple rings, drained and quartered)
4 kaffir lime leaves (fresh or dried)
3/4 cup coconut cream
1/2 cup chicken stock or water
2 tablespoons fish sauce
8–10 basil leaves

Place the pork in a bowl and sprinkle with the cornflour. Add the soy sauce, sherry and sesame oil and stir to combine.

Heat the oil in a large non-stick frypan or wok. Add the pork mixture and stir-fry for 2–3 minutes, then lift it from the pan and set aside, leaving as much oil behind as you can.

Add the onion to the pan and cook, stirring occasionally, until the onion has softened, about 2–3 minutes. Stir in the curry paste and cook, stirring continuously, for about 1 minute, then add the pineapple pieces. Cook, stirring frequently, for a couple of minutes then add the pork, along with the lime leaves, coconut cream and stock or water. Bring the mixture to the boil, then reduce the heat and simmer gently for 5–10 minutes.

Stir in the fish sauce and basil leaves and serve over rice. It might be a Thai-style curry, but Malaysian roti makes a great accompaniment.

Spicy Pork with Peanuts & Noodles

A meal in its own right. This is quick to prepare and can be served hot or at room temperature. If you're working in advance, serve it chilled.

For 2–3 servings:

100–150g bean thread or fine rice
   noodles
1 tablespoon canola oil
1 medium onion, peeled and diced
2 cloves garlic, crushed, peeled and
   chopped
400g minced pork
1 tablespoon red curry paste
1 tablespoon fish sauce
1 cup green beans, cut into 3–4cm
   lengths
1 medium carrot, peeled and finely
   julienned
10–15cm cucumber, deseeded and
   sliced
1/2 cup peanuts
2–4 tablespoons roughly chopped mint
2–4 tablespoons roughly chopped
   coriander

Dressing

2 tablespoons lemon juice
1 tablespoon fish sauce
1 tablespoon light soy sauce
2 tablespoons water
1 teaspoon sugar
1 teaspoon finely chopped red chilli

Place the noodles in a large bowl, cover with the boiling water and leave to stand until softened through (about 5 minutes), then drain.

While the noodles soak, heat the oil in a large pan. Add the onion and garlic and cook for 2–3 minutes, stirring occasionally, until softened. Stir in the pork and curry paste and cook for a further 4–5 minutes, stirring frequently to break up any lumps, until pork is lightly browned. Stir in the fish sauce and beans, cook for a minute or so longer then remove from the heat.

Put the drained noodles in a large bowl, add the carrot, cucumber and most of the peanuts (reserve the rest to use for garnishing). Add the pork mixture and toss to mix.

Make the dressing by combining all the ingredients and stirring until the sugar has dissolved.

Drizzle the dressing over the mixture, add the coriander and mint and toss gently together until evenly mixed. Roughly chop the remaining peanuts and use to garnish just before serving.

Roast Pork Fillets on Caramelised Apple & Onion

Pork fillet is a versatile cut of meat – it is very lean and because even a whole fillet is not very thick, it cooks quickly. This quick roast – with its mix of East-West flavours and techniques – is a good case in point.

I love the combination of five spice powder and pork, but if you're not a great five spice fan, or just don't have any on hand it is still good without it.

For 4 servings:

600–800g pork fillet or fillets
2 cloves garlic, peeled and finely
    chopped
1cm piece ginger, peeled and grated
2 tablespoons Kikkoman soy sauce
1 tablespoon honey
2 teaspoons sesame oil
1/2 teaspoon five spice powder
    (optional)
2 Braeburn or Granny Smith apples
1 medium onion
1 tablespoon honey
1 tablespoon Kikkoman soy sauce
1 tablespoon canola oil

Preheat the oven to 225°C. While the oven heats, put the pork in a large, unpunctured plastic bag and add the garlic, ginger, soy sauce, honey, sesame oil and five spice (if using). Massage the bag so everything is mixed and the pork well coated. Leave to marinate while you prepare the rest of the ingredients.

Core the unpeeled apples and cut each of them into 12–16 wedges. Halve and peel the onion then cut into 5–7mm slices.

Line a roasting pan with a non-stick teflon liner or baking paper. Add the apple wedges, onion, second measures of honey and soy sauce and the oil and toss together until well combined. Remove the fillets from the bag and place on top of the apple mixture, drizzle it with the remaining marinade from the bag, then place in the oven and cook for 20–25 minutes, depending on the thickness of the pork and how well you like it done. The pork is cooked when the juices run clear when pierced at the thickest part.

While the pork cooks, prepare your side dishes, such as the Kumara Mash (see below).

Remove the pork from the oven and leave to stand for about 5 minutes before carving into thick slices. If the apple and onion mixture has not browned, return it to the oven during this time.

Serve the sliced pork on a bed of the caramelised apple mixture, with Kumara Mash and other cooked seasonal vegetables on the side.

Kumara mash

800–900g yellow or orange kumara • 1 tablespoon canola or olive oil • 1 clove garlic, crushed, peeled and chopped • 2 teaspoons grated ginger • 1½ cups hot water • 25g butter • about ½ cup milk or water, if required • salt and pepper to taste

Peel and quarter the kumara lengthwise, then cut them widthwise into slices about 1cm thick.

Heat the oil in a large pot, add the garlic and ginger and cook, stirring frequently, for a minute or so, then add the kumara and water. Cover and boil, stirring occasionally, for about 10–12 minutes, until the kumara is soft.

The water should have almost evaporated when the kumara is cooked, but if there is any left, drain it off and collect it. Add the butter to the pot and mash the kumara, thinning with some of the reserved liquid, and/or the additional milk or water if required. Season to taste with salt and pepper.

Spring Rolls

I think everyone loves spring rolls, and the wrappers can be found in the frozen foods sections of most larger supermarkets or specialty Asian food stores, so why not have a go at making them yourself.
If you don't like the idea of deep frying them, brush them with oil and bake in a very hot oven.

For 8–12 rolls (3–4 servings):
1 tablespoon canola oil
2 cloves garlic, crushed, peeled and
    chopped
2 tablespoons chopped fresh ginger
250g pork mince
150g peeled prawns
1 medium carrot, peeled and grated
1 cup thinly sliced cabbage
110g can sliced bamboo shoots
3–4 spring onions, thinly sliced
2 tablespoons oyster sauce
1 tablespoon soy sauce
1 teaspoon sugar
2–3 teaspoons cornflour
2 tablespoons cold water
8–12 spring roll wrappers, thawed
canola or other vegetable oil to fry or
    brush

Heat the first measure of oil in a large non-stick pan. Add the garlic, ginger and pork mince. Cook, stirring frequently to break up any lumps, for about 5 minutes or until the pork mince has lost its pink colour, then remove the pan from the heat.

Tip the pork mixture into a large bowl and add the prawns, carrot, cabbage, bamboo shoots and spring onions. Stir to combine then add the oyster sauce, soy sauce and sugar and mix thoroughly.

Mix the cornflour and water together and set aside.

Place a wrapper on a clean dry board with one corner pointing towards you (like a diamond). Place 3–4 tablespoons of filling in a line just below the halfway mark. Don't be too generous or they will be hard to roll and may burst during cooking. Fold the bottom corner of the wrapper up so it covers the filling, brush the exposed parts of the wrapper with the corn flour and water mixture, then fold the two 'edge' corners in to make an envelope shaped package. Starting from the bottom, roll the package up to form a cylinder, brushing the flap with a little more cornflour-water mixture to seal if required. Repeat this process until all the filling has been used.

Heat 3–4cm of oil over a medium-high heat in a wok or pot and fry 2–3 rolls at a time, turning occasionally, for 4–5 minutes or until golden brown, then drain on paper towels. Or, alternatively arrange the rolls on a teflon or baking paper-lined oven tray, brush generously with oil and bake at 225°C for 15 minutes.

Serve with steamed rice, and Asian-style vegetables like bok choy, broccolini, or Sesame Cabbage (see page 86).

Teriyaki Pork & Vegetable Stir-fry

This main dish can comfortably be prepared in less time than it takes for the rice to cook.

For 2–3 servings:
400–500g pork schnitzel
1 tablespoon cornflour
2½cm piece ginger
2 cloves garlic
1 medium carrot
1 small head of broccoli
150–200g mushrooms
2 tablespoons canola oil
2 tablespoons water
2 tablespoons Kikkoman soy sauce
2 tablespoons mirin (or white wine)
1 tablespoon brown sugar
1 teaspoon sesame oil
1–2 tablespoons chopped coriander
   (optional)
salt to taste

Cut the pork schnitzels widthwise into 1cm strips. Place in a bowl and sprinkle with the cornflour. Toss together until the pork is evenly coated.

Remove any tough skin from the ginger and cut it into thin slices, then cut these into matchsticks. Crush, peel and chop the garlic, then add with the ginger to the pork. Slice the carrot thinly, cut or break the broccoli into small florets and halve, quarter or thickly slice the mushrooms, depending on their size and set aside.

Heat the oil in a large frypan or wok, then add the pork mixture and stir-fry until it is lightly browned. Remove the pork with a fish slice, place in a bowl and cover to keep warm. Add the carrots and broccoli to the pan and stir-fry until the broccoli is bright green then add the mushrooms. Stir-fry for a further 1–2 minutes, then add the pork back to the pan. Quickly measure in the water, soy sauce, mirin or wine, brown sugar and sesame oil. Toss so everything is well coated then cook, stirring frequently, for 2–3 minutes until the sauce has formed a shiny glaze. Remove from the heat and add the coriander (if using) and season with salt if required. Serve immediately over steamed rice.

Five Spiced Pork on Fried Noodles

The smell of five spice powder in this dish always makes me think of Chinese-style barbecue pork.

For 2–3 servings:
1 medium (300–400g) pork loin
1 tablespoon light soy sauce
1 tablespoon honey
1 tablespoon sesame oil
½ teaspoon five spice powder
200g fine egg noodles
2–3 tablespoons canola or other oil
1 medium onion, peeled, halved and
   sliced
2 medium carrots, julienned
¼ medium cabbage, thinly sliced
2 tablespoons light soy sauce
1 teaspoon sesame oil
hoisin or char siu sauce to serve

Using a sharp knife, lightly score the surface of the pork fillet in a diamond pattern. Place it in a plastic bag and add the first measure of soy sauce, honey, sesame oil and five spice. Massage the bag to mix the marinade, then gently but firmly bang the bag with a rolling pin or the side of a meat hammer until the pork is about half its original thickness. Roll up the bag so the fillet is covered with the marinade and set aside while you cook the noodles in plenty of lightly salted boiling water. When the noodles are cooked, drain them well and set aside.

Heat 2–3 teaspoons of the canola oil in a large non-stick frypan. Remove the pork fillet from the bag reserving the marinade. Shake any excess marinade from the pork and place in the pan. Cook for 5 minutes per side, then remove from the pan and cover to keep warm.

Add another tablespoon of canola oil to the pan, then add the onion and fry until it is soft. Stir in the carrots and cook, stirring frequently. When the carrots begin to soften, add the cabbage and stir to coat with the oil.

Add the noodles and toss the vegetables to mix, adding the remaining canola oil if the noodles look dry. Squeeze the reserved pork marinade into the pan, then add the second measure of soy sauce and sesame oil. Cook, stirring frequently, for 2–3 minutes longer.

Divide the noodles between bowls, slice the pork and arrange on top. Drizzle a little hoisin or char siu sauce over the top before serving.

Chocolate & Hazelnut Friands

If you go back to their French roots, friands were made using ground almonds, so no doubt using hazelnuts instead is some sort of outrageous culinary heresy, but I think I might actually like these even more. On the other hand, maybe its just the addition of the chocolate…who really cares. All that matters in the end is that they're good.

For 12 friands:

1 cup (140g) toasted hazelnuts
100g dark chocolate, melted
25g butter
3/4 cup sugar
1 teaspoon vanilla essence
1/4 cup milk
3 eggs
1/4 teaspoon salt
1/2 cup self-raising flour
6–12 squares (30–60g) chocolate
(optional)

Preheat the oven to 180°C. Place the hazelnuts in a food processor fitted with a metal chopping blade and process until they are ground to the consistency of fine breadcrumbs.

Melt the chocolate by heating in a bowl over boiling water or by microwaving on medium (50%) for 2–3 minutes, stirring after every minute. Add the butter and stir until it melts, then add the ground nuts, sugar, vanilla essence and milk and mix until well combined.

Separate the eggs, stirring the yolks into the hazelnut mixture, and putting the whites into another large clean bowl (any traces of fat will prevent the whites fluffing up). Add the salt, then beat the whites with an egg beater until they form stiff peaks.

Sprinkle the flour over the whites, then pour or spoon in the hazelnut mixture and gently fold everything together just enough to combine.

Thoroughly non-stick spray 12 friand or muffin pans (it pays to do this carefully because they do seem to have a tendency to stick) and divide the mixture between them. Place in the oven and bake for 12–15 minutes until the centres spring back when pressed gently. If you want to add a chocolate centre (particularly good if serving warm) bake the friands for 4–5 minutes, then with the tray still in the oven gently press 1/2–1 square of chocolate (or equivalent) into the top of each, then bake for a further 8–10 minutes.

Remove from the oven and leave to cool for 3–5 minutes (this makes them easier to remove) before turning them out of the pans and cooling on a rack.

Serve after dinner (or anytime really) with coffee.

Note: *To toast the hazelnuts, tip them into a sponge roll tin and place them in the oven as it heats. Keep a close watch on them, as nuts can burn quickly, and remove them from the oven as soon as they have darkened visibly. If you want, you can remove the papery skins by rubbing the nuts and blowing on them, but because the muffins are dark anyway, it doesn't really matter.*

Raspberry & Vanilla Friands

Friands seem to be rapidly gaining in popularity. I don't know whether they will ever completely replace muffins in our psyche or kitchens, because they are a bit more fiddly to make, but they are delicious and make a good occasional treat.

For 12 friands:
100g butter, melted
1 cup ground almonds
1 cup sugar
1 teaspoon vanilla essence
1/4 cup milk
3 eggs
1/4 teaspoon salt
1/2 cup self-raising flour
12–24 fresh or frozen raspberries

Preheat the oven to 180°C. Melt the butter in a medium-sized bowl. Add the almonds, sugar, vanilla essence and milk and stir until well combined.

Separate the eggs, stirring the yolks to the almond mixture and putting the whites into another large clean bowl (any traces of fat will prevent the whites fluffing up). Add the salt then beat the whites with an egg beater until they form stiff peaks.

Sprinkle the flour over the whites, then pour or spoon in the almond mixture and gently fold everything together just enough to combine.

Thoroughly non-stick spray 12 friand or muffin pans (it pays to do this carefully because they do seem to have a tendency to stick) and divide the mixture between them. Place one or two raspberries on the top of each, then place in the oven and bake for 12–15 minutes until golden brown and the centres spring back when pressed.

Remove from the oven and leave to cool for 3–5 minutes (this makes them easier to remove) before turning them out of the pans and cooling on a rack.

Velvety Chocolate Cups

If you're a chocolate lover (or even if you're not) give these really simple chocolate treats a go. We have a set of very small espresso cups (each holds 60–80ml) which are ideal as it is a very rich mixture and you really only need a little at a time!

They take only minutes to prepare, but the catch is they really need to be made several hours (the night before is ideal) before they are required so they will set.

For 4–6 servings:
1 cup milk
200g dark cooking chocolate
1 large egg
1 tablespoon orange liqueur
   (Cointreau etc.)

Put the milk in a medium pot and heat gently until it just boils. While the milk heats, cut or break the chocolate into pieces.

Remove the milk from the heat and add the chopped or broken chocolate and stir until the chocolate has melted. Break the egg into a small bowl, beat it lightly with a fork, then add it to the chocolate mixture along with the liqueur.

Stir the mixture gently until thoroughly combined, then pour it into four to six small cups or ramekins. (Try to break any bubbles on their surfaces so when served they are smooth and shiny looking.)

Cover the containers with cling film, then place them on a tray and refrigerate for at least three hours before serving. (The mixture will keep getting firmer if refrigerated for 8–12 hours).

Serve with coffee and a biscuit or two as the way to round off a meal.

Star Attractions

I could have called these split pastry shapes with berries and cream – although it's descriptive, somehow it doesn't have nearly the same appeal!

When I first made these, I just cut the pastry into rectangles and used plain whipped cream, but over a year or so, with a few more refinements they have evolved into something much more impressive looking while still remaining very simple to make.

For 4 servings:

1 sheet pre-rolled frozen flaky pastry (about 150g), thawed

2 cups berries, single variety or mixed strawberries, raspberries or blueberries

1–2 tablespoons caster sugar

2 tablespoons orange juice

250–300ml cream

1–2 tablespoons caster sugar

finely grated zest of ½ an orange

2–3 drops vanilla essence

Icing sugar to dust

Preheat the oven to 200°C. While the oven heats, cut the pastry shapes. Star shapes make these look extra special (just cut by hand around a cardboard template if you don't have a star cutter big enough) but if you're in a rush, rounds, rectangles (you can get six servings from a sheet with rectangles), or any other shape for that matter, taste just as good. Arrange the pastry on a baking sheet and chill until the oven is ready, then bake for 5–6 minutes until puffed and golden brown. Remove from the oven and cool on a wire rack. (You can do this well in advance if you like.)

Hull and halve or quarter any large strawberries, then place the fruit in a medium-sized bowl. Sprinkle in the sugar (start with the smaller amount and add more if required) and orange juice, then stir gently to combine.

Pour the cream into a large bowl, add the second measure of sugar to taste, the orange zest and vanilla, then beat or whisk until softly whipped (will just hold its shape but does not look dry).

Assemble just before serving by carefully splitting the pastry shapes into two layers. Place the bottom layer on a flattish plate or bowl and cover with a generous spoonful of the berries. Top the berries with a dollop of cream, then carefully place the pastry cap on top. Dust with icing sugar (put a little in a fine sieve and tap or shake gently) and serve.

Orange 'Syrup' Cakes

This is a really easy and versatile cake. It can be made and served in a number of different ways. Make it as a single 20cm ring cake and enjoy it dusted with icing sugar or with orange icing, or take the little extra time needed to soak it with the syrup to transform it into a really special dessert as one large cake or baked in plain or fancy muffin tins for individual servings.

For six individual cakes or one 20cm ring cake:

1 cup sugar
½ cup canola (or other) oil
2 large eggs
finely grated zest of 1 medium orange
½ cup freshly squeezed orange juice
1 teaspoon vanilla essence
½ teaspoon salt
1½ cups self-raising flour

Orange Sugar Syrup

¾ cup hot water
¾ cup sugar
finely grated zest of ½ an orange

Preheat the oven to 170°C (160°C if using fan bake). Measure the sugar, oil, eggs and orange zest into a food processor and blend until pale and creamy. Add the orange juice and vanilla essence and whiz again, then sift in the salt and flour. Mix just enough to make a fairly smooth batter.

Divide the batter evenly (about ½ cup in each) between six non-stick sprayed plain or fancy muffin tins or other moulds (each should hold about 1 cup) or pour into a non-stick sprayed 20cm ring tin. Bake the little cakes for 15–20 minutes or until golden brown and a skewer poked into the middle comes out clean (or 25–30 minutes for the ring tin).

While the cake/s cook prepare the syrup by mixing the hot water, sugar and orange zest together in a small microwave bowl or pot. Heat in the microwave for about 3 minutes on high (100%) or on the stove top, stirring occasionally, until the mixture boils and the sugar dissolves.

Remove cake/s from the oven. Stand for 2–3 minutes before inverting onto a plate or tray and removing the tin. Drizzle the syrup evenly over the bottom and sides of the hot cake/s (about 2 tablespoons per little cake).

Leave to stand for at least an hour (overnight is good), before cutting and serving with lightly whipped cream, ice cream or yoghurt.

Quick Kiwifruit Tiramisu

If you're willing to buy a block of Madeira cake or sponge the most time-consuming part of this delicious dessert is peeling the kiwifruit.

From a traditionalists point of view, calling it tiramisu is probably a bit of a stretch but most of the elements are pretty similar in a kind of deconstructed way.

For about 8 servings:
8–12 green or gold kiwifruit
caster sugar (optional)
300g (about 1¼ cups) mascarpone
1 tablespoon brandy, coffee or orange
   liqueur
¼ cup caster sugar
1 cup cream, lightly whipped
4 teaspoons instant coffee
1 cup sugar
½ cup hot water
400–500g Madeira cake (or sponge),
   cubed
shaved or grated chocolate to garnish

Peel the kiwifruit, then quarter them lengthwise and cut into 7–10mm-thick slices. Sprinkle with a little caster sugar to sweeten slightly if desired.

Put the mascarpone in a large bowl and stir in the brandy or liqueur and caster sugar (this should soften it nicely) then fold in the lightly whipped cream. Cover and set aside until required.

Stir the instant coffee, sugar and water together in a small pot (or microwave bowl). Bring to the boil and simmer for 2–3 minutes (or heat for about 3 minutes on high (100%)) until the sugar dissolves. While the syrup cools, cut the madeira cake into 1–2cm cubes. Place cubes in a shallow dish or tray and drizzle with the syrup, turning them gently so most sides are covered with syrup.

Arrange the sponge, kiwifruit and cream in alternate layers in individual glasses or other containers. Vary the order as you please, if you put sponge at the bottom it soaks up any excess liquid nicely. If you finish with a layer or dollop of the cream mixture, it looks great garnished with a little shaved or grated dark chocolate. (If desired, you can assemble these, except for the final layer, up to 8 hours in advance. Just cover and refrigerate until required.)

Crème Brûlée

Crème Brûlée is an unashamedly rich dessert! As such, I think it is best served in fairly small quantities – I have a set of four little white ramekins, which hold just over half a cup each that I think make a good serving size, but in fact it could easily fill six slightly smaller dishes and still be satisfying.

If you don't like the idea of using cream only, you can use a mixture of equal parts cream and milk. Interestingly, the full cream version sets a little firmer than the milk and cream version, so in some ways the latter can actually seem creamier in the mouth.

For 4–6 servings:
2 cups cream (or 1 cup cream and
   1 cup milk)
2 vanilla pods (optional)
4 large egg yolks
1/2 cup sugar
1 teaspoon vanilla essence
1/8 teaspoon (pinch) salt
4–8 teaspoons caster sugar

Preheat the oven to 150°C. Pour the cream (or milk and cream) into a small pot or microwave bowl. Add the vanilla pods (if using) and heat gently until it just boils.

Place the egg yolks, first measure of sugar, vanilla essence and salt in another bowl and whisk together.

Remove the vanilla pods (if used) then pour the hot cream mixture into the bowl and whisk again. (If you did use the vanilla pods, you can split them lengthwise, gently scrape out the tiny black seeds and add these to the mixture too.)

Pour the mixture through a sieve to remove any lumps, then carefully pour into the four to six ramekins, leaving a few millimetres at the top of each. Arrange the ramekins in a sponge roll tin or roasting pan and carefully pour in enough hot water to fill to about halfway up the outsides of the ramekins.

Place the tin or pan in the oven and bake at 150°C for 25–30 minutes or until the custard has just set (it will still appear a little jiggly, but not runny), then remove them from the oven.

Brûlées are versatile and can be served while still quite warm in cool weather, or in warmer weather (or if you are working in advance) cool to room temperature or even refrigerate until required. Just before serving, sprinkle the top of each ramekin evenly with 1–2 teaspoons of caster sugar (the smaller quantity for small ramekins or more for larger ones).

Arrange the ramekins on a tray and place under a very hot grill (3–5cm from the heat) for 2–3 minutes until the sugar melts and browns. (You can do this with a blowtorch if you have one.) Remove from the heat and let the caramelised sugar cool and harden to form a crisp layer, then serve immediately.

Variations: *If you like coffee, try adding 1/4 cup whole roasted coffee beans instead of (or as well as) the vanilla pod. The beans will be removed when the mixture is sieved, but you can add two or three of the collected beans to each ramekin before baking. The just-baked custard has a mild coffee flavour, but this intensifies on standing.*

Extra Easy Apple Tartlets

If you use pre-rolled pastry sheets for these, the most complicated part is really peeling and slicing a couple of apples! I have given quantities for 4 servings as this is what you get from one pastry sheet.

For 4 servings:
1 pre-rolled sheet flaky pastry
2 tablespoons walnut or pecan pieces
1 tablespoon caster sugar
½ teaspoon cinnamon
2 medium apples (Granny Smith,
    Braeburn or Cox's Orange)
3–4 tablespoons apricot jam, warmed

Sit the pastry on a lightly floured board to thaw and preheat the oven to 190°C (180°C if using fan bake).

Measure the nuts, sugar and cinnamon into a food processor or blender and process until the nuts are finely chopped.

Peel, then halve and core the apples (or core, then halve the apples if you have a corer). Lie each half on a board and cut into slices 2–3mm thick. Depending on the size of the apple you should have 15–20 slices.

Cut a 2cm wide strip from one side of the pastry sheet so you are left with a rectangle. Cut this into four (equally sized) smaller rectangles and arrange these on a baking sheet. Without cutting right through, run a sharp knife 1cm in from the edge of each rectangle so it marks out a frame. Spread 1–2 teaspoons of the sugar-nut mixture over each piece of pastry leaving the border clear, then carefully fan out a sliced apple half on each.

Warm the apricot jam (about 30 seconds in the microwave) and brush a little over the whole of each tartlet. Bake for 15 minutes or until the pastry is golden brown. Leave to stand for 5–10 minutes, then brush with a little additional warmed jam and serve.

Maple-Pecan Loaf

I like loaves, they tend to be simpler than cakes to make because the butter (or in this case oil) and sugar don't need to be creamed, and they can be eaten in different ways.
*   Served warm, a thick slice topped with a dollop of whipped cream or ice cream, and perhaps a dribble of maple syrup makes a great dessert. When it has cooled it can be sliced and eaten plain or buttered, with tea or coffee, or added to school lunches.*

For 1 medium (12 x 25cm) loaf:
½ cup maple (or maple flavoured)
    syrup
½ cup canola oil
½ cup milk
1 large egg
½ teaspoon salt
2 cups self-raising flour
½ cup lightly packed brown sugar
½ cup roughly chopped pecans
    (or walnuts)
½ cup sultanas
1 teaspoon cinnamon
½ teaspoon mixed spice

Preheat the oven to 160°C. Measure the first five ingredients into a large bowl and whisk together until well combined. Measure in the remaining ingredients, then stir until just combined.

Pour mixture into a teflon or baking paper and/or non-stick sprayed loaf tin and bake for 35–40 minutes until firm when pressed in the centre and skewer comes out clean. Remove from the oven, leave to stand for a few minutes then remove from the tin and cool on a rack.

Serve warm with a dollop of whipped cream or ice cream or cool, plain or buttered.

Filo Cased Rhubarb-Cream Tarts

If I was asked what my favourite childhood dessert was, I would probably have to say it was my mother's Rhubarb Cream Pie. Obviously, from the name, these little tarts are a tribute to her version.

For 4 servings:
1 large egg
1/2 cup sour cream
1/4 cup sugar
1 teaspoon vanilla essence
4 sheets filo pastry
1–2 tablespoons canola oil
4–6 sticks (about 150–200g) rhubarb

Preheat the oven to 170°C. Break the egg into a medium-sized bowl. Add the sour cream, sugar and vanilla essence, then whisk until smooth.

Lie the stack of four filo sheets on a clean, dry board. Cut the stack into quarters (giving four equally sized smaller rectangles) so you have a total of 16 small sheets. Stack these up and cover with a clean dry tea towel to prevent them drying out.

Lightly oil or non-stick spray four individual pie plates (each about 10–12cm across). Working one pie plate at a time, gently press one small sheet of filo into the bottom of the plate, brush it very lightly with oil, then add another sheet turning it a little so the corners point in a different direction. Repeat this process until the shell is four layers thick. You don't need to brush the inside of the last layer with oil, but do brush all the protruding edges to help ensure even browning. Repeat this process to give four tart shells.

Cut the rhubarb into 2–5cm lengths and arrange it evenly between the shells. Pour a quarter of the sour cream mixture into each tart. Arrange the tarts on a large tray and place in the oven. Bake for 15 minutes or until the crust edges are golden brown and the filling has set.

Remove from the oven and leave to stand until just warm (or completely cool) before serving with a dollop of softly whipped cream on the side.

Coconut & Lemon Loaf

This is a quick, versatile and, perhaps most importantly, great tasting loaf. Like any loaf it can be sliced and eaten as a snack with tea or coffee, but sliced and served warm with a spoonful of lemon honey (see below) and a dollop of cream, or a scoop of vanilla ice cream, it becomes an interesting dessert.

For 1 medium (25 x 12cm) loaf:
1 lemon
1 cup sugar
1 large egg
¼ cup canola oil
½ cup milk
1 teaspoon vanilla
2 cups desiccated coconut
1 cup self-raising flour
1 teaspoon baking powder
½ teaspoon salt
about ¼ cup shredded coconut
    (optional)

Preheat the oven to 160°C. Using a potato peeler, thinly peel the yellow zest from the lemon. Place the strips of zest and sugar in a food processor fitted with a metal chopping blade and process until the zest is chopped finely through the sugar. (Alternatively, finely grate the zest and mix with the sugar in a large bowl.)

Add the next four ingredients, plus the juice of the lemon and process (or whisk) until pale and creamy looking. Sprinkle in the coconut then sift in the flour, baking powder and salt. Process in very short bursts, or mix very gently, until just combined. (Don't worry if it looks very wet, the coconut will soak up some of the liquid during cooking.)

Pour mixture into a lined 25 x 12cm (8 cup capacity) loaf tin, sprinkle the top with about ¼ cup of long coconut shreds for decoration if desired. Bake for 30–40 minutes until golden brown and a skewer poked into the middle comes out clean. (Loosely cover the top with baking paper or foil if it is getting too brown before the middle is cooked.)

Remove from the oven, leave to stand for a few minutes before removing from the tin and cooling on a wire rack. Serve with Lemon Honey and whipped cream or ice cream.

Lemon Honey
3 lemons • 1 cup sugar • 50g butter • 3 eggs

Finely grate the zest from two of the lemons, then squeeze the juice from all three. Place the grated zest and sugar in a small microwave bowl or pot with the cubed butter. Strain in the lemon juice, then lightly beat the eggs and strain these in too.

Stir everything together then microwave on high (100%) for 1 minute bursts, stirring between each, until the sugar has dissolved and the mixture has thickened. (Or heat very gently on the stove top, stirring continuously, to the same end point).

Use immediately or transfer to clean jar, seal with a lid and store in the fridge for 1–2 weeks.

Bok choy

Green vegetable with long, white, fleshy stems topped with dark green crinkly leaves, also known as 'pak choy' and 'Chinese chard'.

Broccolini

Cross between broccoli and the Asian green, gai larn. It has long, thin stems and small florets.

Cannellini beans

Small, white kidney beans, popular in Tuscan cooking, available dried (soak overnight before cooking) and in cans – great to keep on hand in the pantry.

Char siu sauce

Sometimes also called 'Chinese barbecue sauce'. Thick, sweet and salty, it is quite similar to 'Hoisin sauce' (they can be used interchangeably if required). Keeps almost indefinitely in the fridge.

Chiao tzu wrappers

Also known as 'gow gee wrappers' these are very thin (1–2mm) pastry rounds 8–10cm in diameter. They tend to be very pale or white in colour (as opposed to won ton wrappers which are quite yellow) and turn semi-transparent as they cook.

Chined

A term referring to the removal of the backbone (or chine) from a cut of meat, e.g. a chined rack of lamb has had the bone between the chops removed to facilitate carving.

Daikon

Also known as 'Chinese white radish', these are white and range from the size of a parsnip or very large carrot to about 50cm long and 15cm thick.

Hoisin sauce

Thick, slightly sweet and spicy, brownish-red sauce made from fermented soya beans, flour, sugar, vinegar, spices, garlic and chilli.

Hokkien noodles

Thick, yellow, egg noodles sold fresh in plastic bags (from the refrigerator) in Asian food stores, health-food shops and supermarkets.

Julienne

To cut into very thin sticks; mostly applies to root vegetables such as carrots, and sometimes meat and poultry.

Kaffir lime

A variety of lime producing a dark green (relatively juiceless) fruit with a knobbly rind. The fragrant leaves are widely used in Thai and Malay dishes. If possible look for fresh leaves, but if unavailable use dried leaves instead – if these can't be found lemon leaves can be used instead.

Mascarpone

A very thick, 'double-cream' dairy product. Technically qualifies as a cheese but has a sweet, rich, cream-like flavour, used fresh in savoury and sweet dishes.

glossary

Mirin
Sweet rice wine with a low alcohol content, used in cooking and for glazing foods.

Porcini mushrooms
Highly prized Italian creamy brown mushrooms, mostly available in dried form.

Portobello mushrooms
A variety of the common field mushroom, their caps tend to be brownish, rather than creamy and when fully open are about 10–12cm across.

Sumac
Dark purplish-red berries with a sharp fruit flavour, available dried or ground and used in the Middle-East and North Africa.

Shiitake mushrooms
Rich brown mushrooms with curled-under edges, available fresh from some markets but often available dried from supermarkets or Asian food stores (sometimes labelled 'Chinese black mushrooms').

Star anise
Small, dry, brown seed-cluster, shaped like an eight-pointed star, with a aniseed-like flavour.

Surimi
A cooked and processed fish product (often made with New Zealand hoki), popular in Japan and other parts of Asia. The interior is white in colour (sometimes the outside is dyed reddish orange) with a mild, slightly sweet flavour. Sometimes it is also moulded, coloured and flavoured to resemble crab meat or even lobster tails.

Szechwan peppercorns
Dried reddish-brown berries that release a sharp, spicy fragrance when roasted and ground. Also known as 'Chinese pepper' and 'fagara'.

Tahini
Creamy paste made from ground sesame seeds, often used in Greek and Middle Eastern dishes.

index

weights & measures

The recipes in this book have been tested using a standard metric (250ml) measuring cup. All cup measures are level, unless otherwise stated.

In New Zealand, South Africa, the USA and England, 1 tablespoon equals 15ml. In Australia, 1 tablespoon equals 20ml. These variations will not adversely affect the end result, as long as the same spoon is used consistently, so the proportions are correct.

Grams to Ounces and vice versa

General	Exact
30g = 1oz	1oz = 28.35g
60g = 2oz	2oz = 56.70g
90g = 3oz	3oz = 85.05g
120g = 4oz	4oz = 113.04g
150g = 5oz	5oz = 141.08g
180g = 6oz	6oz = 170.01g
210g = 7oz	7oz = 198.04g
230g = 8oz	8oz = 226.08g
260g = 9oz	9oz = 255.01g
290g = 10oz	10oz = 283.05g
320g = 11oz	11oz = 311.08g
350g = 12oz	12oz = 340.02g
380g = 13oz	13oz = 368.05g
410g = 14oz	14oz = 396.09g
440g = 15oz	15oz = 425.02g
470g = 16oz	16oz = 453.06g

Recipes based on these (International Units) rounded values

Liquid Measurements

25ml	(28.4ml)	= 1 fl oz		
150ml	(142ml)	= 5 fl oz	= $\frac{1}{4}$ pint	= 1 gill
275ml	(284ml)	= 10 fl oz	= $\frac{1}{2}$ pint	
425ml	(426ml)	= 15 fl oz	= $\frac{3}{4}$ pint	
575ml	(568ml)	= 20 fl oz	= 1 pint	

Spoon Measures

$\frac{1}{4}$ teaspoon	= 1.25ml
$\frac{1}{2}$ teaspoon	= 2.5ml
1 teaspoon	= 5ml
1 tablespoon	= 15ml

In NZ, SA, USA and UK 1 tablespoon = 15ml.
In Australia 1 tablespoon = 20ml

Measurements
cm to approx inches

0.5cm = $\frac{1}{4}$"	5cm = 2"
1.25cm = $\frac{1}{2}$"	7.5cm = 3"
2.5cm = 1"	10cm = 4"

Cake Tin Sizes
cm to approx inches

15cm = 6"	23cm = 9"
18cm = 7"	25cm = 10"
20cm = 8"	

Oven Temperatures

	Electricity		Gas Mark
	°C	°F	
Very cool	110	225	$\frac{1}{4}$
	120	250	$\frac{1}{2}$
Cool	140	275	1
	150	300	2
Moderate	160	325	3
	180	350	4
Moderately Hot	190	375	5
	200	400	6
Hot	220	425	7
	230	450	8
Very Hot	240	475	9

Abbreviations

g	grams
kg	kilogram
mm	millimetre
cm	centimetre
ml	millilitre
°C	degrees celsius

American-Imperial

in	inch
lb	pound
oz	ounce